THE
HUMAN JESUS
IN THE
GARDEN
OF
GETHSEMANE

JOHN H. DUMKE, SR.

ISBN 978-1-63575-235-9 (Paperback)
ISBN 978-1-63575-236-6 (Digital)

Christian Faith Publishing, Inc.
296 Chestnut Street
Meadville, PA 16335
www.christianfaithpublishing.com

Printed in the United States of America

CONTENTS

INTRODUCTION

I can relate to Joseph's comment in Genesis 50:20 when he was speaking to his brothers about their sin of selling him into slavery many years before.

> *But as for you, ye thought evil against me; but God meant it unto good, to bring to pass, as it is this day, to save much people alive. (Gen. 50:20)*

_IN 1989_ Another man and I started a business preparing living trusts for our insurance clients (we also owned an insurance agency), but we made a mistake. Following the advice of our attorney, we didn't file a form in the state of Missouri for an exemption from the securities department as we had already filed with the S.E.C. in Washington D. C. This was necessary because we were raising capital for our company.

That omission was all the legal profession needed for the lawyers we had angered with our business, which was costing them millions of dollars in probate fees, to force us to close the business. We lost the business, our home, our credit, and good name—all we owned personally; and eventually we were forced to file for bankruptcy.

That still didn't satisfy them, so criminal charges were brought against me! After a sham of a trial in an obscure village run by the "good old boys," I was sentenced to two six-year sentences and was given a $200,000 fine!

They, the attorneys, meant this for evil. But God meant it for good!

Pain

There is a pain that goes so deep,
it numbs the brain, disrupts the sleep.
Starts with a drip somewhere below,
becomes a torrent, a gushing flow.

I see an eddy, a whirlpool black,
the vortex is drawing, pulling me back.
Emotions swirl, gain power and speed,
away from light, to blackness they lead.

Where are my friends, my loved ones dear?
What happened? Tell me! Why am I here?
I guess life's over, give up, and drown.
The black hole encloses, as I go down.
See nothing, hear nothing, say nothing at all,
people speak, don't hear them, while I fall.
The world is silent, all movement is slow,
Slipped out of my mind, I've let myself go.

I don't hurt, or feel pain anymore.
My mind has numbed me; it knows the horror.
It doesn't matter what you do to me,
my body's Novocain has set me free.

I have no strength to fight the pull
of depression's hole, filled to the full.
It starts to turn my head from the light
I succumb as I enter depression's dark night.

Wait! I hear! I feel, no, can almost see,
your hand, no two, reaching down tome.
One grabs me with strength, power and might,
one touches and loves me, erasing the night.

My heart had stopped; beats again,
life that was over, revived, begins.
Your love brings light, chases the black,
God's power, redeems and brings me back.

Thank you, I needed that.

For as long as I can remember, I've been running away from what I always knew God wanted me to do—serve Him. While in prison, alone, God had my attention; and I became willing to do His will. It took a while for my obedience to become willing obedience, but God is patient.

Our precious Lord met every need, every month, for my wife Nita Raye and our youngest son Christopher, who although almost thirty years of age, in love and compassion, put his own life on hold and stayed at home to help his mother while I was away.

There was no way in the natural world for them to meet the bills on their combined income, yet they were met each and every month. This monthly miracle started with a simple commitment from Nita Raye.

*"Father, we will do the very best we can and look
to you to provide what we need over and above our
income to meet our obligations."*

God honored that request and met every need, every month, until they had the income to do it on their own!

That commitment was the beginning of many lessons God taught me through his precious give of love, Nita Raye, my wife.

During these long lonely months, the Holy Spirit gave me more than a hundred poems, a number of children's stories and several book subjects. *The Majesty, the Mystery and Mission of Marriage*, now available at amazon.com, was the first book published and the *Garden* is the second one, and as I read them now, I realized I didn't write them. The Holy Spirit did. I simply held the pen and let His words flow through me. I am blessed every time I read the words, and I pray you can step into the teaching and allow God's Spirit to minister to you as well.

I dedicate this writing to my Lord Jesus Christ and his love for us, without which none of us could survive this life of pain.

*It is of the LORD's mercies that we are not con-
sumed, because his compassions fail not. They are
new every morning: great is thy faithfulness. (Lam.
3:22–23)*

I also want to thank some of God's children for their faithfulness in "visiting" me while in prison, some in person some by letter and\or phone calls but all gifts of love. First I want to thank my parents, Rev. Allen and Mae Dumke for their twice a week letters, as well as their love and childhood training, which I drew upon daily for strength while in prison. (Dad and Mom have finished their work, and are now and forever with the Lord.)

I want to thank our children, Kim, Stephanie, John Junior, Bradford, James and Christopher for standing with me and believing in me. I want to thank my brothers Allen and David my sister Darlene my other sister, (sister-in-law) Susan; my mother-in-law Gram, my aunt Loraine, as well as many other family members and friends who sent prayers and love. A special thank you to our friends of over fifty years, David and Barbara Gaetke, who came from Las Vegas Nevada on several occasions to visit me. They wrote often and sent money to my prison account frequently, as did Nita and our children, so I could buy a few extras, as well as needed items from the canteen.

(Susan, Gram, Aunt Loraine, and Barbara are all enjoying their rewards in heaven.)

Most of all I want to thank and honor the most wonderful lady in the world—Nita Raye, my love, my wife. Not once during this horrific time did she rail at me or blame me for our situation or turn her back on me, as so many wives do when their husbands are in prison. I know, I spent much time with rejected men, comforting and praying with them. I could write a book about Nita Raye's love, devotion, and support and may one day. For now, I will share with you what the Holy Spirit gave me about her one night as He sees things from the spirit world.

"When I couldn't lift the bitter cup God gave me to drink, she picked it up, cradled my head in her arms and put it to my lips like a mother administering medicine to her child. She helped me drink it to its final dregs, speaking words of love and comfort, soothing my troubled mind."

"When tears came and blurred my vision, she became my eyes and led me through 'till I could see

again. When I Said I felt abandoned! She stood tall and vowed, "I haven't left you and I never will!"

"Little did I realize at the time, that while I was drinking my bitter cup, so was she; when tears blinded me, she blinked hers back so we both could see; when I felt abandoned, I'd abandoned her, yet she stood in the gap for me until I had the strength to stand again by her side.

There is no person whom I respect or honor more. She is the personification of a good and Godly wife.

She is my hero, Nita Raye, my wife.

PREFACE

We all know the story of the garden of Gethsemane, but I believe most of us have thought of it in terms of Jesus as the Son of God doing what the Father wanted him to do without question, not recognizing that Jesus the Son of Man, which was His favorite name for Himself, was fighting the desires of his humanity. In this discourse, we will take a look into the human soul of Jesus and correlate His experiences and decisions to us in our times and perspective to see how these lessons He learned can affect us today in our decisions of life. It is the belief of the author that the thought starters brought forth will challenge the reader to seek a deeper, more productive walk with our Lord as he/she looks into and surrenders to walk through their own personal garden of Gethsemane.

Jesus was and is God, but for a time and a purpose, he put on the cloak of humanity and wept like we do for the suffering of others and finally for his own impending trial and anguish. Jesus, as God, knew what was coming and had prepared himself for it from the foundation of the world. He was ready to rescue all humanity from Satan's lair. Jesus, the human son of man, had to overcome the humanity in his garden of Gethsemane before he could accomplish his godly task on Earth.

All of us have events in our lives that spiritually we have prepared for, yet when the trial presents itself, we try to avoid it. Jesus prayed three times at an hour each time to have this horrific event taken from Him instead of having to go through it. Yet in the end, He accepts it for you and me and the joy beyond.

CHAPTER 1

THE HISTORICAL GARDENS

For a number of years my wife Nita, our son Chris, and I lived on an acreage just outside of Arlington, Nebraska. One of the things we liked most about our little country estate was the nursery, a tree farm of about 160 acres owned by a local nursery company that was directly across the road from us and which we used as our own private woods to walk the dogs, our yellow Labrador retrievers Sundance and Annie. Actually, if the truth were known, the dogs ran and we walked. I suppose the idea of grown, supposedly intelligent people, walking their dogs while living in the country begs the question, Why? Well, we did not allow the dogs to cross the road alone (Sometimes they did anyway, but if we didn't catch them, it didn't count in their eyes), so it was a real treat to run and chase rabbits they never caught, birds who flew away, and any other critters they could scare up.

It was also a very special time for us to be alone with God. I can remember praying for guidance, for our special needs and those of our family, which was growing with marriages and grandchildren. Then came a time of crying out to God for understanding of events occurring that were not in our plans and were tearing at the very fabric of our lives and destroying everything material we had worked for and asking—no, pleading—for a closer, deeper, and more powerful walk with Him.

This is where he taught me to praise Him for His blessings and goodness, His love, and His sacrifice on our behalf. Although it would be a while before I would see the benefits available to us for praising Him in "all" things, it was a start toward what would become a different way of life, one of believing that whatever God brought or allowed in our lives was for our good and His glory. Therefore, He was worthy of praise.

When Nita and I walked together, we talked about things married people do, sometimes lost in our individual thoughts of who to blame for the pain of our calamities, not wanting to voice accusations but feeling them anyway. It is hard to be open and affectionate to the one who causes the pain, be it your spouse, family, friends, or even God. Understanding these issues would need time, spiritual growth, and godly wisdom. Sometimes we just enjoyed the closeness that twenty-five plus years of togetherness clothed us with when we are still very much in love. (A 2016 note: we celebrated our fiftieth anniversary on April 14, 2016.)

When Chris and I walked, we would talk about God, fishing, and his future, just as fathers and sons have done since the beginning of time.

All of us need a place like the nursery, a place where we can pray, praise, and be still and know that He is God:

Be still, and know that I am God: I will be exalted among the heathen, I will be exalted in the earth.
(Ps. 46:10)

Jesus had such a place. It was a garden possibly owned by a wealthy believer, perhaps Nicodemus or Joseph of Arimathea; but it is obvious He and His disciples had permission to use it as often as they wanted because it was a favorite quiet place, a place of refreshment and rest for Him, and a place, no doubt, where many conversations took place between Jesus and His Father.

Let's take a trip to this particular garden that played such an important role in Jesus's life and in showing us the humanness of our Lord. May it help us understand why after more than two thousand years, anyone who has heard of Jesus, has also heard of Gethsemane.

As we travel east of Jerusalem, having passed through the eastern gate, we see about a mile away, a limestone ridge running north and south called the Mount of Olives. This was another favorite resting and teaching place of Jesus, and on the way, we will pass many gardens, one will be just across the Kidron Valley, two hundred yards or so from the city's eastern gate, the site of many great events in the earthly life of Jesus, the garden of Gethsemane. There really was nothing to set it apart from any other garden except it *was used by Jesus.*

That is a lesson in itself, isn't it? The difference in gardens or people is whether God is allowed to use them. Someone said, "God is not looking for your ability. He is looking for your availability."

In my life it seems that I was willing to let God have me when I wasn't busy doing other more important things. "I know what you said, Lord, but I really need to get this project finished first. And remember, I gave my word on this other program, Lord. And I know you wouldn't want me to break my word, and if nothing else comes up that might interfere, I'll be available for service the first of next year. I hope that's okay with you. Oh, by the way, Lord, You do remember what I am believing You for. Remember Your word, Lord, I'm standing on it. I know You won't let me down!"

Sound like anyone you know? God's promises are conditional whether we like it or not. They are conditional on our *willing obedience.*

God does not owe us anything. We owe God everything. We owe Him our very life and breath. Stand back, look at your priorities. Is God's Word and will number one in your life? Or are you fitting Him in somewhere between 10:30 p.m., after the news, sports, weather, and your fall-asleep time? I know all about doing that because I did it for years until God put me in a situation that demanded spending time with Him and His Word to remain sane. And God will do that, or something like it to any of us, if that's what it takes to get our attention. He is far more interested in our eternal home than our current comfort. Perhaps it is priority evaluation time in your life as it was in mine.

The Mount of Olive comes into the first century with quite a history.

> *And David went up by the ascent of mount Olivet, and wept as he went up, and had his head covered, and he went barefoot: and all the people that was with him covered every man his head, and they went up, weeping as they went up. (2 Sam. 15:30)*

Here is the story of King David escaping to the mountain from his son Absalom, who attempted an overthrow of the kingdom. David wept bitterly for the evil that had befallen his house due to the sin committed with Bathsheba:

> *Thus Saith the LORD, Behold, I will raise up evil against thee out of thine own house, and I will take thy wives before thine eyes, and give them unto thy neighbor, and he shall lie with thy wives in the sight of this sun. (2 Sam. 12:11)*

For thou didst it secretly: but I will do this thing before all Israel, and before the sun. (2 Sam. 12:12)

David cried unto God in sincere repentance, and God brought a great victory and great blessing, but not without cost. David learned that the price of sin is great and bitter. But when we repent, it opens the door for our loving Heavenly Father to take the worse things we do, the things that cause a stench that fills His nostrils, and make those things into the best soil in our garden, if we repent and trust Him with praise on our lips and trust, total complete and absolute trust, in our hearts. God uses a "composting" process to perfect us, and it is the heat of the affliction or trial that causes the foul garbage of our lives to become His best soil.

If we are to experience the oneness with Him that we all say we want and that we sing about in our hymns, we must allow the refining process. We must allow God to remove the dross of our lives, so the pure gold of Jesus's life being lived through us can be seen and used by our Savior for our good and His glory.

This is a prayer the Lord gave me while on house arrest in St. Joseph Missouri, after spending three years, one month, and one day in prison.

"Help me, Lord, today, to help someone else along their way, to give them hope when all seems lost, to strengthen and encourage each life storm tossed, to show your love by caring, to give myself in sharing, and to reflect your love so all can see I'm just being to them what you've been to me."

Here is recorded another great sin of one of David's sons. The mount is where Solomon, as king, built "high places" for his wives so they could offer sacrifices to their gods. Because of this abomination the place became known as the mount of corruption.

Then did Solomon build an high place for Chemosh, the abomination of Moab, in the hill that is before Jerusalem, and for Molech, the abomination of the children of Ammon. (1 Kings 11:7)

Solomon would not allow the altars of foreign gods in the City of God out of respect for Jehovah, but he would not rid his life or his kingdom of them in deferring to the wishes of his pagan wives and to appease his own appetite, even though it meant defying Gods laws. Where did he learn to do this? From his father Adam! Yes, Adam! This is precisely what Adam did. He violated God's law to stay in communion with his wife! The Bible says Adam sinned, not Eve, she was beguiled. Today we would say she was tricked.

Let me share with you what I see. When Eve offered the fruit to Adam, he saw what had happened. Eve had a dead spirit, not a living one like he had and like she had before her disobedience, and he realized in that most pregnant of all moments that he had to make a decision. What a decision! If he refuses to follow Eve's transgression, he *may* lose her forever. He will have to go to God his Father and "tell" on his wife and God will have to deal with her.

Or had you ever considered what God would have done if Adam had gone to his Father and stood in the gap for her? Would God have acted according to his nature and loved or allowed Adam to love her back into fellowship? Isn't that what Jesus did for man just in a different way? Adam knows if he follows Eve he will have to turn his back on God his Father, and I believe with the living spirit of wisdom God had given Adam, he knew the awful consequences of that decision.

But for want of the human relationship of his wife and, more importantly, to become like God, and because he did not trust God to solve his, God's, problem (if Adam lacked the wisdom or knowledge to solve this problem or to answer the questions raised, he knew God could), he did it anyway, much to both his and the whole human race's regret. Furthermore, the sin was his because he wasn't "beguiled" as Eve was. He was enticed with the "lust of the flesh, the lust of emotions, and the pride of life."

The Spirit of God gave me this picture of the operation of pride.

Pride

I probably should just keep my mouth shut, about me, I mean. But here is the problem. I am the spirit of pride, and as such I want everyone to know everything I do and to give me the glory I so richly deserve. But if you know who I am and what I do, will you stop allowing me to control you?

The answer is, of course not!

Why?

Because I and only I of all the spirits (I know you call us demons) have the ability to hide myself and all I do in your life from you! Therefore, you *will* keep doing all the prideful things I want you to and will either believe you are being humble or at least never think of yourself as being controlled by me. Rather, you will justify all your actions as your way of being reasonable or proper. Whether you believe it or not, most of my best subjects are sitting in a church pew every Sunday morning and appear to be the most humble of all the people there.

You may ask where I came from, and that is a legitimate question. After all if everything He created was good in His eyes and He considers me to be evil, then either He created evil or I used my free will to rebel against Him. Well, I guess you know the answer to that. (I never call Him by the name you do because that would mean I consider Him to be more powerful than me, and I cannot believe that because I plan on replacing Him on the throne of the universe).

Okay then, here is the real story of me, Pride!

I was created to be an expression of satisfaction of doing a good job. You humans even use the phrase, "I take pride in a job well done." He considers that to be a proper response to a job well done, and He uses it all the time. He used it after every accomplishment of His in the history of creation and has reserved it in the welcome speech for each of His servant-sons and daughters when they meet Him in person. He also used the phase in reference to the accomplishments of His Son while on earth. So you see He created it to glorify Himself and then used me to implement it.

I got to thinking and asked myself this question: "Why should I do all the work and He get all the glory?" The more I thought on that question, the more I considered the unfairness of it all. But if I were to do anything about it I would need help. I wasn't powerful enough by myself to challenge Him, but what would happen if all of heaven's population were to rebel? Why, He would have to abrogate the throne and I would be there to take over. This became an obsession with me, and I started looking around for spirits who could be used. As I noticed a reversal in my priorities and an almost fearful expectancy of interaction with Him now that my every thought and plan placed me at the center of my world instead on Him, I reasoned that I must find spirits who had attributes I could use to cause the same reaction in them. "What," I asked myself, "would cause a spirit to rebel against his creator?" Then it struck me! Only me, Pride, could do this. Why, you ask? Remember what I told you before, I hide within myself. Those who embrace themselves above Him embrace me and I control them through themselves, well, really through my spirit, Pride. Beautifully diabolical, don't you think?

My first conquest was to be my most important, and all I used was the truth about a spirit being. He had to be a leader and his attribute had to be visible, not just one of those "inner" things. It had to be something that was now used to glorify Him but through self-examination, self-thought, and self-aggrandizement would turn him against Him.

My first choice was Lucifer. As the "anointed cherub," he sat in the presence of Him. He was the director of the music to celebrate the greatness of Him and he was the most beautiful of all the created spirit beings. All I would have to do was turn his attention inward to himself instead of outward to Him. In order to do that I must find a way to enter into him so I would become a part of him, the controlling part. He must become my vessel. All I had to work with was what he already had, his attributes.

Here is how I did it. You are just going to love this!

I met up with Lucifer after one of the musical celebrations of exalting the greatness of Him, and I said, "Lucifer, how beautiful your music is. He must be very proud of you."

Lucifer replied, "Oh, it isn't my music. God the Father gives it to me, and I just play His song. I am His instrument. I play to glorify Him, not myself."

I needed to set the hook, as a fisherman might say, so I said, "Oh, of course, I know you are doing your part to bring glory to Him and you do an excellent job. But I was just thinking of you, Lucifer. After all you are the anointed cherub. You stand in the very presence of Him. You are the most beautiful of all the heavenly Hosts. You direct the heavenly orchestra. All the other angels admire you. I was just wondering, have you ever wanted to 'play your own song' rather than always playing His?"

I had planted the "seed" of self in his mind. Would it take root? All I could do was wait. I did not have the right to enter into him, to take over his person, without his permission. However, I would take advantage of even the slightest invitation. (The same is true of us.)

He was processing the seed thoughts I had planted.

I waited.

Then he said, "Well, it is true. I am the most beautiful, and I should be entitled to more than the others because of my great beauty, but—"

I never let him finish his thought. I entered into him with just that tiny opening because what he had done was begin to question Him by turning his focus to himself!

In that instant I, through me, Pride, reversed his thoughts and caused him to think of himself first and consider me a friend and colleague and Him as the enemy to his own wants. Lucifer looked at me with a new look. I recognized it. It was the essence of pride, and it looked just like me. He said, "I see now what I must do. Would you help me play my own songs? I need to be heard for what I am. I must direct my life to be all I can be. I will captain my own soul. I am the most beautiful of all the creations of Him, and I make the best music, and many of my friends will help put me on the throne of the universe. I will ascend into heaven. I will exalt my throne above the stars of God: I will sit also upon the mount of the congregation, in the sides of the north: I will ascend above the clouds; I will be like the most High" (Isa 14:13–14).

I smiled within myself and agreed with all he asked, and I settled down within him and took over his will and his life. It was no longer Lucifer who lived but me in him, the hope of my glory.

(John H. Dumke Sr., 9/2006)

When we see a modern man of God fall, let's remember Solomon and let's read what this man chosen of God to lead Israel prayed when dedicating the temple he had built according to God's direction in 1 Kings 8:22–53. What a stirring prayer of repentance for his people and a passionate plea for protection!

I have reprinted it here for all to read and to pray it for our nation, a nation consecrated to Almighty God and protected by Him when we obey Him and His words.

And Solomon stood before the altar of the LORD *in the presence of all the congregation of Israel, and spread forth his hands toward heaven:*

And he said, LORD *God of Israel, there is no God like thee, in heaven above, or on earth beneath, who keepest covenant and mercy with thy servants that walk before thee with all their heart:*

Who hast kept with thy servant David my father that thou promisedst him: thou spakest also with thy mouth, and hast fulfilled it with thine hand, as it is this day.

Therefore now, LORD *God of Israel, keep with thy servant David my father that thou promisedst him, saying, There shall not fail thee a man in my sight to sit on the throne of Israel; so that thy children take heed to their way, that they walk before me as thou hast walked before me.*

And now, O God of Israel, let thy word, I pray thee, be verified, which thou spakest unto thy servant David my father.

But will God indeed dwell on the earth? behold, the heaven and heaven of heavens cannot contain thee; how much less this house that I have builded?

Yet have thou respect unto the prayer of thy servant, and to his supplication, O LORD *my God, to hearken unto the cry and to the prayer, which thy servant prayeth before thee today:*

That thine eyes may be open toward this house night and day, even toward the place of which thou hast said, My name shall be there: that thou mayest hearken unto the prayer which thy servant shall make toward this place.

And hearken thou to the supplication of thy servant, and of thy people Israel, when they shall pray toward this place: and hear thou in heaven thy dwelling place: and when thou hearest, forgive.

If any man trespass against his neighbour, and an oath be laid upon him to cause him to swear, and the oath come before thine altar in this house:

Then hear thou in heaven, and do, and judge thy servants, condemning the wicked, to bring his way upon his head; and justifying the righteous, to give him according to his righteousness.

When thy people Israel be smitten down before the enemy, because they have sinned against thee, and shall turn again to thee, and confess thy name, and pray, and make supplication unto thee in this house:

Then hear thou in heaven, and forgive the sin of thy people Israel, and bring them again unto the land which thou gavest unto their fathers.

When heaven is shut up, and there is no rain, because they have sinned against thee; if they pray toward this place, and confess thy name, and turn from their sin, when thou afflictest them:

Then hear thou in heaven, and forgive the sin of thy servants, and of thy people Israel, that thou teach them the good way wherein they should walk, and give rain upon thy land, which thou hast given to thy people for an inheritance.

If there be in the land famine, if there be pestilence, blasting, mildew, locust, or if there be caterpillar; if their enemy besiege them in the land of their cities; whatsoever plague, whatsoever sickness there be;

What prayer and supplication so ever be made by any man, or by all thy people Israel, which shall know every man the plague of his own heart, and spread forth his hands toward this house:

Then hear thou in heaven thy dwelling place, and forgive, and do, and give to every man according to his ways, whose heart thou knowest; (for thou, even thou only, knowest the hearts of all the children of men;)

That they may fear thee all the days that they live in the land which thou gavest unto our fathers.

Moreover concerning a stranger, that is not of thy people Israel, but cometh out of a far country for thy name's sake;

(For they shall hear of thy great name, and of thy strong hand, and of thy stretched out arm;) when he shall come and pray toward this house;

Hear thou in heaven thy dwelling place, and do according to all that the stranger calleth to thee for: that all people of the earth may know thy name, to fear thee, as do thy people Israel; and that they may know that this house, which I have builded, is called by thy name.

If thy people go out to battle against their enemy, whithersoever thou shalt send them, and shall pray unto the LORD toward the city which thou hast chosen, and toward the house that I have built for thy name:

Then hear thou in heaven their prayer and their supplication, and maintain their cause.

If they sin against thee, (for there is no man that sinneth not,) and thou be angry with them, and deliver them to the enemy, so that they carry them away captives unto the land of the enemy, far or near;

Yet if they shall bethink themselves in the land whither they were carried captives, and repent, and make supplication unto thee in the land of them that carried them captives, saying, We have sinned, and have done perversely, we have committed wickedness;

And so return unto thee with all their heart, and with all their soul, in the land of their enemies, which led them away captive, and pray unto thee toward their land, which thou gavest unto their fathers, the city which thou hast chosen, and the house which I have built for thy name:

Then hear thou their prayer and their supplication in heaven thy dwelling place, and maintain their cause,

And forgive thy people that have sinned against thee, and all their transgressions wherein they have transgressed against thee, and give them compassion before them who carried them captive, that they may have compassion on them:

For they be thy people, and thine inheritance, which thou broughtest forth out of Egypt, from the midst of the furnace of iron:

That thine eyes may be open unto the supplication of thy servant, and unto the supplication of thy people Israel, to hearken unto them in all that they call for unto thee.

For thou didst separate them from among all the people of the earth, to be thine inheritance, as thou spakest by the hand of Moses thy servant, when thou broughtest our fathers out of Egypt, O Lord GOD. (1 King 8:22–53)

This is God's promise of continuity of a son to sit on his throne.

And it came to pass, when Solomon had finished the building of the house of the LORD, and the king's house, and all Solomon's desire which he was pleased to do,

That the LORD appeared to Solomon the second time, as he had appeared unto him at Gibeon.

And the LORD said unto him, I have heard thy prayer and thy supplication, that thou hast made before me: I have hallowed this house, which thou hast built, to put my name there for ever; and mine eyes and mine heart shall be there perpetually.

And if thou wilt walk before me, as David thy father walked, in integrity of heart, and in uprightness, to do according to all that I have commanded thee, and wilt keep my statutes and my judgments:

Then I will establish the throne of thy kingdom upon Israel for ever, as I promised to David thy father, saying, There shall not fail thee a man upon the throne of Israel.

But if ye shall at all turn from following me, ye or your children, and will not keep my commandments and my statutes which I have set before you, but go and serve other gods, and worship them:

Then will I cut off Israel out of the land which I have given them; and this house, which I have hallowed for my name, will I cast out of my sight; and Israel shall be a proverb and a byword among all people:

And at this house, which is high, every one that passeth by it shall be astonished, and shall hiss; and they shall say, Why hath the LORD *done thus unto this land, and to this house?*

And they shall answer, Because they forsook the LORD *their God, who brought forth their fathers out of the land of Egypt, and have taken hold upon other gods, and have worshipped them, and served them: therefore hath the* LORD *brought upon them all this evil. (1 Kings 9:1–9)*

This promise was conditioned on obedience to Gods first commandment

I am the LORD *thy God, which have brought thee out of the land of Egypt, out of the house of bondage.*

Thou shalt have no other gods before me. (Exod. 20:2–3)

In Deuteronomy, God gives the results of obedience and disobedience as follows.

> *And it shall come to pass, if thou shalt hearken diligently unto the voice of the LORD thy God, to observe and to do all his commandments which I command thee this day, that the LORD thy God will set thee on high above all nations of the earth: (Deut. 28:1)*

> *But it shall come to pass, if thou wilt not hearken unto the voice of the LORD thy God, to observe to do all his commandments and his statutes which I command thee this day; that all these curses shall come upon thee, and overtake thee: (Deut. 28:15)*

Man is given the responsibility for his own household, so by allowing his wives to worship other gods, in God's eye, Solomon, the king of God's people, was worshiping other gods! Men, *you* are held responsible for the actions of your household. Whether they be actions of you, your wife, or your children, God sees them as your actions and will deal with you for your disobedience! Think about it!

Chapter 11 finds Solomon disobeying God:

> *Wherefore the LORD said unto Solomon, forasmuch as this is done of thee, and thou hast not kept my covenant and my statutes, which I have commanded thee, I will surely rend the kingdom from thee, and will give it to thy servant. (1 Kings 11:11)*

Because of this sin, God did rend the kingdom from his linage until the Messiah reigns.

Let's not be too hard on Solomon, or fallen soldiers in our day, before we examine our own lives for our "foreign gods" or what is not "clean" enough to allow in our Jerusalem, our home or our business, but that we refuse to rid ourselves of. We all have our compromises, but God hates them and will not allow us to get by with them anymore than He allowed Solomon. Read Ecclesiastes to see the repetitive old Solomon calling everything vanity, yet we know it is not all vanity, only what is of self is vanity, what is of God blesses only. He and only He brings prosperity and no suffering with it.

> The blessing of the LORD, it maketh rich, and he
> addeth no sorrow with it. (Prov. 10:22)

In these final days of the dispensation of grace, I believe the Spirit of God is asking us to examine ourselves closely because judgment always begins at the house of God.

> For the time is come that judgment must begin at
> the house of God: and if it first begin at us, what
> shall the end be of them that obey not the gospel of
> God? (1 Pet. 4:17)

What things are you doing that you want to believe are "allowed" because of our liberty in Christ, that Jesus would object to if you asked Him? What are you doing in secret that you wouldn't do in the light of day? These are the altars that God said must be broken down as were the altars of Solomon in Hezekiah's reign, if we are to enjoy the presence of Jesus in our lives.

Do you feel you receive too much pleasure in your disobedience to "give it up"? If you do, give them up as a sacrifice of "pleasure" and trust God to replace anything and everything we give up or deny our-selves with a gift of far greater value when we willingly in obedience bow our will, our lives, and our appetites to Him.

We will again visit the Mount of Olivet in a later chapter in order to view a dramatic climatic event, but for now let's concentrate on the garden. The garden of Gethsemane gave a very commanding view of the city of Jerusalem, yet it was close enough for a short walk for needed rest or perhaps sleep. In as much as we have no record of Jesus ever spending a night in the city, which will be His capital and from which He will one day rule and reign the whole world, perhaps He did spend many nights sleeping or communing with God in the garden.

Think about it. The God of the universe who created the stars, sleeping under them, enjoying their beauty as I'm sure He did in the day He created them. The garden—a place of rest; a place to pray and to talk with His dear Heavenly Father; the place that will become His place of decision, submission, and obedience. For us it is the same, it is our place of resting in God and prayer that God makes our place of decision!

There is no escaping it. God demands it. His peace has a price, and that price is always the same for everyone "born of woman"—submit to Him, deny self, keep your eye single, and keep it focused on the glory beyond the problem. That glory is victory here on earth and eternity with Him.

In 1973 Nita and I had the privilege of visiting the western part of Croatia, which was at that time Yugoslavia. Many of the natives live just as the people have for hundreds of years, in the hills with donkeys as transportation. Simple people living from the fruits of the land much like the people in Jesus's day. How different from the hustle and bustle of our lives, and dare I say, better in some ways. The countryside is much the same as parts of Palestine with rocky hills, meadows in valleys, olive gardens and vineyards; and I felt an awesome fellowship with Jesus and His disciples thinking, *This must be what the world looked like to Him.*

I could visualize the Master walking along one of the winding paths followed by His band of disciples, passing through fields, skirting the walled vineyards and gardens, preaching the good news of the kingdom, His kingdom, the kingdom of love and forgiveness and praise. Even His disciples did not really hear Him they only heard what they wanted to hear, just like us, always listening, never hearing.

> *Therefore speak I to them in parables: because they*
> *seeing see not; and hearing they hear not, neither*
> *do they understand. (Matt. 13:13)*

We all need a "garden," a place of rest and a place to rest, a place of peace, a place to pray, and a place to hear from our Heavenly Father. If you don't have a place like this now, by all means find one or create one and begin visiting often for your peace and communion with God. This practice will change your life. Jesus showed us how to have real power for service.

> *And in the morning, rising up a great while before*
> *day, he went out, and departed into a solitary*
> *place, and there prayed. (Mark 1:35)*

It wasn't by being in the noise and the crowds. It was by separating himself to be alone with His Father, to be energized by God's power to be able to minister amid the noise without being influenced by it. Without this quiet time, we become caught up in the demands of hurt and hungry people and our own self-importance, and then we risk falling like King Saul did when the Holy Spirit left him and he did not notice.

But the Spirit of the LORD departed from Saul, and an evil spirit from the LORD troubled him. (1 Sam. 16:14)

And Saul was afraid of David, because the LORD was with him, and was departed from Saul. (1 Sam. 18:12)

We have seen that happen in our day to ministers, as well as neighbors, friends, family, and, at times, ourselves.

Now therefore thus saith the LORD of hosts; Consider your ways. (Hag. 1:5)

Questions:

1. Do you have a quiet place to spend quality time with God?
2. Are you going to find one and use it?
3. Is it priority evaluation time for you? Take time to meditate on this and let God's Holy Spirit help you.
4. What things or attitudes do you need to give to God so He can turn them into the best soil in your garden?
5. What foreign gods or altars have you set up that need to be cast down?
6. What things are you doing because of your liberty in Christ that you need to stop because of the damage to your relationship with Him?

Activity:

Make a *private* list of all the garbage in your life and ask God to turn it into the best soil in His garden!

CHAPTER 2

SETTING THE SCENE: JESUS' LAST WEEK

God the Holy Spirit allows two gaps of time in Jesus life where we know nothing of his activities. We see his miraculous conception, birth, eighth-day circumcision, fortieth-day dedication, with its prophesies in the temple, then about two years later.

> *Now when Jesus was born in Bethlehem of Judaea in the days of Herod the king, behold, there came wise men from the east to Jerusalem,*
>
> *Saying, Where is he that is born King of the Jews? For we have seen his star in the east, and are come to worship him.*
>
> *When Herod the king had heard these things, he was troubled, and all Jerusalem with him.*

And when he had gathered all the chief priests and scribes of the people together, he demanded of them where Christ should be born.

And they said unto him, In Bethlehem of Judaea: for thus it is written by the prophet,

And thou Bethlehem, in the land of Juda, art not the least among the princes of Juda: for out of thee shall come a Governor, that shall rule my people Israel.

Then Herod, when he had privily called the wise men, enquired of them diligently what time the star appeared.

And he sent them to Bethlehem, and said, Go and search diligently for the young child; and when ye have found him, bring me word again, that I may come and worship him also.

When they had heard the king, they departed; and, lo, the star, which they saw in the east, went before them, till it came and stood over where the young child was.

When they saw the star, they rejoiced with exceeding great joy.

And when they were come into the house, they saw the young child with Mary his mother, and fell down, and worshipped him: and when they had opened their treasures, they presented unto him gifts; gold, and frankincense, and myrrh.

And being warned of God in a dream that they should not return to Herod, they departed into their own country another way.

And when they were departed, behold, the angel of the Lord appeareth to Joseph in a dream, saying, Arise, and take the young child and his mother, and flee into Egypt, and be thou there until I bring thee word: for Herod will seek the young child to destroy him.

When he arose, he took the young child and his mother by night, and departed into Egypt:

And was there until the death of Herod: that it might be fulfilled which was spoken of the Lord by the prophet, saying, Out of Egypt have I called my son. (Matt. 2:1–15)

After Herod's death, we have the record of their return and settlement in the city of Nazareth in Galilee (vs. 23). This is where Joseph and Mary had lived growing up, but Joseph had planned to live in Judea, possibly Bethlehem after the baby was born in order to protect Mary from the local gossip of the fact she was with child before Joseph married her. However, he was warned in a dream (vs. 2:22) by God to return to Nazareth.

Then several years later we have the record of Jesus's first trip to the temple in Jerusalem at the age of twelve (Luke 2:42–52) and the account of him debating with the doctors of the law. When his parents realized he wasn't with their friends or family, after they had departed for home, they went back to Jerusalem and spent three days searching the city for him. They finally found him in the temple and scolded him for lagging behind. He said, "How is it that ye sought me? Wist ye not that I must be about my Father's business?"

In these questions, he was notifying his earthly parents that he understood his mission on earth. There is something else he is saying that I missed in all the times I had read this scripture and had heard it preached. Maybe you saw it, but I didn't. Jesus expected his parents to know that if he wasn't with them he would be in the temple. "Why would you look anywhere else for me, except the temple? Where were you looking for three whole days?" It wasn't a disrespectful question. It was a question of wonderment. These were the people who had known who he was and where he had come from since before he was born. So if anyone would or should know where he would be it was them.

We are told in the same passage that he went home with them and was obedient to them as his parents. Jesus was the perfect example of obedience, first to his Heavenly Father, then to his earthly parents. It is fruitless for us to try to attribute childhood miracles as some have done to him. It should suffice to take only what the scriptures say:

> *And he went down with them, and came to Nazareth, and was subject unto them: but his mother kept all these sayings in her heart. (Luke 2:51)*

Have you ever thought about the fact that God very carefully chose the parents he wanted for his son? And he also very carefully chose your parents specifically for you. Why? Ask Him!

We don't hear from or about Jesus again until he was ready to begin his ministry with his water and Spirit baptism as recorded in Matthew chapter 3.

This is how I see the events of his life before Jesus left home.

When Jesus the Carpenter Became Jesus the Christ
The Day Before

The widow brought a tray of cakes, some dates, and a pitcher of wine to her boys in their carpentry shop. She set it down and told them to take a break, rest, and refresh themselves. The oldest son, Joshua, smiled and said, "Thank you, Mother. Come on, brothers, as father used to say, when mother brings a reason to rest it must mean we need it."

The boys, men all, with the oldest just now thirty shook the wood chips and dust from their garments and sat down to eat. There was the normal shop talk of which jobs would be completed, when and what was coming up to be done, then almost as if a new train of thought was introduced, Joshua spoke to the next oldest, James, "I will go to Gaius's place this afternoon to complete our agreement and to lay out the position of the barn he wants built. You need to start taking materials to him tomorrow. Our other work should be done before this Sabbath so his can be started next week. Oh, and James, I have the books all brought up to date in father's desk. You'll know what to do to collect our pay at harvest time."

Joses said, "Joshua, you sound like you won't be here to help build the barn."

Joshua replied, "Well, if all other work is done by weeks' end and if you two plus Simon and Jude will work together, you can complete Gaius's barn on time without me. And, James, just make sure Mother receives my share of the profits, as well as her own."

With that, Joshua stood up, ending their rest and the conversation and went back to work on his project, which brought Simon to say, "He gets more like father every day. He won't answer our questions if he doesn't want to."

After the noon lunch Joshua left the shop and walked north out of town to Gaius's place. He always enjoyed these times of solitude. It gave him a chance to meditate on the word of God and to recite the Psalms. He also spent time in prayer, sort of walking and talking with God.

Gaius had been a good friend of their father and his son Lucius had been Joshua's friend for as long as he could remember, although on this day Lucius was not home but on a trip for his father. Gaius said he expected him home on the morrow. Although they were Greek and their Hellenistic culture was evident in all they did and said, they nevertheless had accepted Jehovah as their God and were converts due to the life and witness of Joshua's father.

Gaius worked with Joshua to lay out the position of the barn, and then they completed their arrangements. The barn would be paid for with grain at harvest time. This was the normal type of payment, but that meant there were times Joshua and his brothers had to wait for payment due to poor crop yields or a prolonged rainy season. In fact they had even had to help with more than one farmer's reaping just to make sure the grain made it into the barns before bad weather set in or they could not have been paid.

By the time Joshua got home the sun was setting, the shop was closed, his brothers were gone, and his mother had supper ready for him.

It seemed to him that she had prepared a special meal for this night, almost a feast. She waited until he was finished eating, then started a rather nostalgic conversation. It began with the often related story of his birth, how very special he was, and the joy she had experienced being his mother all these years. There were pauses when each in their own way mused on the past. There was laughter at some of the silly things they had experienced and some of the joys. Joshua interjected his thoughts and perspectives in a way he couldn't remember doing before. His mother seemed to particularly enjoy his comments. She continued through each phase of her life, recalling the trials and triumphs ending with the day she became a widow. She sighed then with a loneliness only known to those who have lost a loved one.

Joshua listened, letting the evening unfold. It seemed to him she needed to do this just now, and perhaps, just perhaps, he needed to as well.

Does she know? Does a mother know when her son is about to leave home?

At last Joshua arose and said, "Mother, I need to walk awhile. I feel a need to pray." He hugged his mother, wrapped his cloak about his shoulders, and disappeared into the night.

Well, after midnight, the front door creaked and Joshua quietly slipped over to his sleeping place. As he spread out his mat, a low moan escaped his lips and he groaned obedience, "Yes, Father, I will. I know it's time."

His mother awoke with the door creak and then heard her son's prayer, spoken in pain. She quietly arose, opened a drawer, and removed a package. She laid it on top of the chest her husband had made so many years ago as a wedding present.

She lay back down to await the morning and her son's announcement. Then she whispered her prayer: "Yes, Lord God, I know it's time. Thank you for lending him to me. I give him back to you now."

It seemed as if a sword pierced through her own soul as she wiped the tears from her eyes.

Sleep did not come to either of them that night, only an occasional drifting in and out of a twilight rest until morning.

It was time.

The Morning

Joshua awoke from one of his twilight dozes but waited to open his eyes. It was that frozen moment in time, just before the darkness of night was required to flee chased by daylight. It was his favorite time. The rooster would crow the signal for all God's singers, the birds, to try to outdo each other singing praises to their creator. To open one's eyes now seemed to him to profane the moment. The other senses would be subdued if sight were allowed to reign. How could he smell the dawn if his eyes were open? It was as if God made special air, brand-new air, for smelling at dawn. And the sounds of dawn! Of course everyone heard the birds. The soft twitting of a summer's afternoon that could lull a shepherd to sleep came from the same throat as the screaming of dawn. They sounded like an orchestra tuning up before playing the concert of daytime melodies. The other sounds he listened for were the gifts of patience at dawn's first light, the insects' sounds, some nondescript, others musical. He listened for the cows asking to be milked, the she goats with the same request, the bleating of lambs wanting breakfast, the braying of a donkey, and the distant cry of a hawk on the wind searching for food to feed its young. Each animal in turn announced its entrance into the world of awareness.

Then there were the mother sounds. He wondered if he had ever in his life awakened before her. In thirty years, he couldn't remember even one time. He knew she had already started a fire, made the dough, and had the breakfast cakes in the oven. He could smell them. When he sat down, everything would be ready as it always was.

Wait, not yet. Take one last breath. Inhale deeply. Live for one more moment in the breathless, sightless wonder of the sounds of dawn. At last he opened his eyes to this new day. He was blessed with a window that faced east just above where he slept, and as he did every morning, he stood before it to enjoy the rising of the sun.

"Thank you, Father, for again allowing me the joy of your presence and the glory of your creation."

He stood for a long time this morning, absorbing the beauty and drinking the nectar of dawn.

At last he rolled up his mat, stowed it away, and stepped outside. When he returned, he washed his face and hands and prepared for breakfast.

"Good morning, Mother." He gave her a hug and kissed her cheek. Although she had been a widow for some time now, was still young enough, and very attractive, she was adamant about not remarrying. Her children had encouraged her to find someone to spend her later years with, but her response was always the same: "Who could ever replace your father!" Finally, the children gave up, honored her decision, and no one mentioned it anymore.

Her daughters had all married and were busy starting their families as had her sons, all that is except Joshua. Now it was just mother and son, and they had drawn even closer to each other.

One element of their earlier family life continued. Their mother insisted on the "boys" having lunch with her each day since the shop was connected to her house and it was the family business. It made her feel like they still lived at home.

Now as Joshua sat to eat with his mother, they bowed their heads and Joshua prayed,

"Almighty God, Jehovah, who provides all things for life, we honor you, we give you glory. We pray for your will to be done in our lives and hearts even as you have purposed in heaven. Supply all we need for this day. Forgive us as we forgive others. Lead us in the paths of righteousness and deliver us from all evil. We give you all praise and honor forever and ever, amen."

As Joshua began to eat, his mind recalled all the mornings of all the years they had eaten together as a complete family. Father, mother, and a house full of children. Where had the years gone?

When he was a child it seemed he'd never be a man. Now as a man, it seemed he'd never been a child, that childhood had been a dream. *Such is life bounded by time*, he mused.

Recalling his childhood, he remembered traveling a great deal. He supposed, now that he was older, the trips had been much harder on his parents than they had been on him. But even now he found little pleasure in those memories. He enjoyed life much more after they settled in their village and the carpentry shop was opened. Some of his clearest early memories were of being in the shop with his father playing in the wood chips and later learning the trade with his father's guidance. While they worked on the different projects, the conversation was always directed to first include and then be dominated by the scriptures. His father knew more scriptures and could recite more of them for his children's benefit than any man Joshua had ever known.

As was the custom, at the age of eight, he began his instruction at the synagogue and had shown an extraordinary interest in the Torah. How he loved the stories of the history of his people, especially the settlement of the Promised Land. However, no matter how exciting those adventures were there was no question that the writings in the book of Psalms were his favorite. Over the years he had become a very learned expounder of the scriptures and was called upon many times to read in the synagogue. Now that he had reached the age of thirty, he would be asked to teach in the weekly assembly as well.

His mind seemed to be continuing the nostalgic travels of last evening only without the interplay of conversation with his mother

He recalled his bar mitzvah, his first trip to the Temple in Jerusalem with his parents, his questions to the priests, and each trip thereafter. He reviewed his life in a panorama of times and events not stopping until today.

His mother, noticing his silence, spoke first. "Son?"

"Yes, Mother."

"Is everything all right?"

"Yes, Mother. The business is going well. Jude and James will be here soon and will finish Eli's plow today. Samuel's yoke will be done tomorrow, and they will start on Gaius's barn next week with Simon and Joses."

Joshua continued to give an inventory of the planned work of the business, not that she would be personally involved but rather to reassure her that her income from the business would be sufficient to meet her daily needs.

Again, there was a long silence.

Finally, after he was finished eating, he leaned back a bit and with the start of a frown on his brow he said, "Mother. Today I must be about—"

Mary interrupted him with, "I know, son. I've known for some time. I've been waiting for you to tell me. Wait here a moment for your mother's sake. I have something to give you before—" With that she left the room and went into her sleeping quarters and emerged with her package of love. In anticipation of this day, she had woven a one-piece cloak of white linen for her son. Oh, how long and tedious this labor of love had been, but worth it all now as she presented it to him, holding it out in front of her like an offering to God.

He took it carefully, unfolding it and letting her help him drape it over his shoulders.

"Son, you will need this against the cold of the nights."

Joshua turned his back so she could adjust the cloak and to hide the tears in his eyes. Had any mother ever loved a son as much as his loved him?

My mother. God's love was greater true, but when
I look into her eyes, I see his love shining through.

"Mother, I don't know when—"

She interrupted again. "God knows. I'll be here when you want to see me. I've always known this day would come. I've never feared it, though it seems to me to have come too soon. I'll miss you very much, but I'll see you again. For now, I know you must do what Jehovah has called you to do."

Joshua put his arms around his mother, held her close for a few moments, and thought, *Why does this woman of strength seem so frail now?* Then he turned and walked out the door. He didn't look back. He walked through the town, seeing things that had gone unnoticed on other days but now were things he wanted to remember. He drank in each scene and each memory, savoring it and saving it for future recall.

He climbed the hill out back of the village, and as he had done so many times in the past, he looked out over the pleasant land.

Joshua had become fluent in Hebrew, Aramaic, and Greek due to the location of their village. Unique in time, their village stood at the crossroads of ancient trade routes from Tyre and Sidon on the west and old caravan roads from Damascus on the northeast. They were a halfway house between Damascus and Egypt, Antioch and Jerusalem. Here, competing cultures met, brought by traveling merchants with their goods and travelers from Rome. Additionally, from the west came the caravans loaded with the cargo of the ships that unloaded at the seaport, Caesarea. King Herod the great had started building the city a half century ago, and it took twelve years of intense labor to complete. He had spared no expense using the finest architects and engineers of his kingdom and meant for it to be a monument to Caesar. It had wide underground passageways for transporting carriages and pedestrians alike from the center of town to the magnificent beaches of the great sea. There were the theaters, the hippodrome, and, of course, the marble temple Herod built to honor his god, Caesar.

From the north stretching down into Egypt, were the military roads bringing messengers with news from Rome. Sometimes they carried good news, sometimes bad, but always with an effect on the people of the occupied lands of Rome's conquests.

Mount Carmel in the distance reflected the sun's rays and seemed to offer glory to God as a reminder of the day Elijah called down fire on the water-soaked offering and demanded of the apostate children of Israel, "If God be God, worship him!" From antiquity, the triumph of Elijah rang out as clear as the day the children shouted Jehovah's praises as they helped Elijah slay the four hundred prophets of Baal. He looked to the north at Mt. Tabor and remembered the judge Deborah had sent Barak and ten thousand men against Sisera, the captain of Jabin's army, with his nine hundred chariots and a multitude of soldiers; and God gave them a great victory. His heart felt the pain of loss as he recalled that King Saul and three sons died in battle against the Philistines on Mt. Gilboa to the south. His eyes continued further south to the area known as Samaria and wondered at the animosity between their two peoples. Samaritans, the descendants of the "mixed" multitude who came from Egypt with the Israelites, who walked with them for forty years in the wilderness, were now shunned by them. To the east was the Sea of Galilee with its ring of hills appearing to protect it from the outside world. Herod Antipas, the procurator of Galilee, had built a palace for himself in the hills overlooking the western shore of the sea where the city of Tiberius was built as a tribute to the current ruler in Rome. Herod Antipas was the son of Herod the Great and half-brother of Philip, the procurator of eastern Galilee, and also of Herod the Tetrarch of Judea.

It was about twenty-eight years ago that their father had all male children two years old and under killed in and around Bethlehem to protect his kingdom from the possible birth of a new king of the Jews. Another great embarrassment to the Jews was that Herod and

his son, the kings of the Jews, weren't even Jews, but Edomites, enemies of the Jews! A shudder shook his body as he thought on the
cruelty of man to his fellowman

Joshua turned his back on his country's past and started his
descent eastward to the river Jordan. He was going to Beth-barah
on the other side of the Jordan, some three-day's journey south not
far from the city of God. He had received news from travelers out
of Jerusalem of a prophet proclaiming the coming of the "anointed
one," the Messiah, and baptizing those who came to him repenting
of their sins against God. His message was, "Repent for the Kingdom
of Heaven is at hand!"

He had planned to follow the river south, staying away from
crowds and off the main highway, the one Rome had built to connect
Tiberius with Jericho, in order to have time alone with God, then to
pass over to the east bank of the Jordan near Beth-barah to find the
prophet. However, as he approached the highway he recognized his
friend Lucius on the way home from the trip for his father. It would
be an insult not to stop and greet him though he wanted to be on his
way. The men greeted each other. Lucius always called Joshua by his
Greek name, although no one else in town did. Joshua smiled at his
friend's quirk. They visited about Lucius's just-completed trip and
Joshua's just-begun one.

Then as the urgency was there to be on his way, Joshua ended
their conversation with, "Lucius, my friend, I must continue my
journey. There is still a way to go before dark. I have an appointment
with my kinsman John the day after tomorrow and must not tarry.
Take care, my friend, until we meet again." He hugged his friend and
turned to go.

Lucius called after him, "Peace, and may our God prosper your
way, my friend, Jesus!"

The Trip to Beth-Barah

"Yes, Father, I will do your will as a man, only as a man."

Jesus rose from his knees, stretched, and walked around for a while, not praying any longer yet in communion with His Father. Periodically the words, "Yes, Father" would escape, His lips punctuating the stillness of the night. Occasionally He would lift His eyes to stare fixedly at some distant point in the night sky, which seemed to be visible to Him although there was nothing the naked eye could fasten on.

At last He lay down and wrapped His cloak about Him for protection from the cool night air and thanked His mother aloud for her gift of love.

Sleep came for rest's sake, though He thought He would have preferred to continue His communion with His Father.

The second day of travel was a repeat of His first. Then the day of destiny began.

The first rustling of leaves moved by the pre-dawn breeze, which God sends to wake the warblers, His heralders of day, woke Jesus to this day of destiny. As His eyes opened, His heart and lips continued His earlier communion with His Father. He had traveled about half the distance from Nazareth of Galilee to the place He would cross over the Jordan to where His kinsman, John, was preaching and baptizing, a place near Beth-Barah. He had one cake left in His lunch pouch from home. After giving thanks He took a bite and searched for berries. Finding some He picked a handful and enjoyed the blending of tastes. The sweetness took His mind back to home and the memories of the preserves his mother would offer for breakfast. He thanked her aloud for the memories and love.

Jesus walked the last leg of his journey south to the road connecting Jericho on the west to the Jordan River and Beth-Barah on the east with a determined step, a lively gait, and joined the crowd, unnoticed, coming to hear the prophet who many believed to be the Messiah. He listened to their conversations with interest. There were the ever present Roman soldiers making sure no rebellion was afoot. And they all walked and talked together.

One traveler asked another, "Do you suppose this John is starting another revolt like the one started by that Judas of Galilee some years ago?"

Someone answered, "I don't think so. John talks of God and a Kingdom of Heaven and our coming Messiah, not rebellion against Rome."

One man asked no one in particular, "Is he the Messiah?"

Another answered, "He says no, but rather he is making the way straight announcing the Messiah's coming."

"Is He alive now? I mean the Messiah."

"Well, John thinks so! He's looking for Him every day."

"What does the Prophet do? What does he say?"

"He preaches repentance toward God and doing good and not evil."

"Why is King Herod so angry with John?"

"Because John has criticized Herod for taking his brother Phillip's wife, Herodias, as his own and for not obeying the laws of God."

"Doesn't John realize Herod could have him killed for what he has said?"

"I'm sure he does, but that doesn't seem to affect him."

So, the conversations continued, one asking questions, others, who had already heard John's message, answering as they brought friend and family to hear what they had heard.

The air of excitement was thick with the expectation of the Messiah. No prophet had arisen for over four hundred years in Israel. The devotees were hungry with a spiritual hunger that superseded even physical hunger, and it pleased Jesus.

The closer they drew to the prophet the greater the number of the curious, as well as the devoted. Today John was surrounded by his disciples, men who fancied themselves his protectors, men who had left their homes and livelihoods to hear his words and to be a part of the prophet's ministry, just as men have done for centuries when God raised up a prophet. The leaders of the synagogue may hate them, even kill them, but they followed their prophets regardless the cost because they loved them and it made them feel closer to God.

Preparation for Ministry

Jesus drew close to the river were John was baptizing and took His place in line with those who had been convicted in heart and desired to change their lives. He stood there waiting to be baptized. One after another John admonished, then immersed the people in the River Jordan, then sent them on their way. He saw the tears of repentance, the joy of reconciliation, and rejoicing in God their Savior.

Then Jesus stood in front of John. John knew who He was before He spoke. The Holy Spirit within him reacted, just as He had at their first meeting while John was still in his mother's womb.

> *Then cometh Jesus from Galilee to Jordan unto John, to be baptized of him.*
>
> *But John forbad him, saying, I have need to be baptized of thee, and comest thou to me?*
>
> *And Jesus answering said unto him, suffer it to be so now: for thus it becometh us to fulfil all righteousness. Then he suffered him.*
>
> *And Jesus, when he was baptized, went up straightway out of the water: and, lo, the heavens were*

opened unto him, and he saw the Spirit of God
descending like a dove, and lighting upon him:

And lo a voice from heaven, saying, this is my
beloved Son, in whom I am well pleased. (Matt.
3:13–17)

The Jewish custom that he had instituted under the law or old covenant allowed a man to teach in the temple services after he reached the age of thirty. That is when Jesus began his ministry. Jesus always followed and obeyed the law but seldom any of the man-made traditions. This above all other things he did upset the religious leaders of his day.

Although we could discuss Jesus's earthly ministry at length, we will leave that for another time, as our purpose is to get to the garden. However, there is one incident I would like to bring to the attention of the reader as recorded in Matthew 4:11. After his forty-day fast and fending off the temptations of Satan, he received strength from the angels.

Then the devil leaveth him, and, behold, angels
came and ministered unto him. (Matt. 4:11)

Did you know that we can receive the same angels ministering to us. In the depths of our greatest challenges, when we do not know where to turn, God sends His angels to minister to us.

Be not forgetful to entertain strangers: for thereby
some have entertained angels unawares. (Heb.
13:2)

Question: How is it that the Creator of the universe, as well as these very angels who were doing the ministering, had to receive their ministry? Who were they ministering to, the divine God-ness of Jesus or the human-ness of Jesus? Why could he not have used his God-ness to strengthen himself? You remember when Jehovah made his covenant with Abram, he swore by Himself, "For there was no one greater than Himself whereby he could swear" (Heb. 6:13). So why not minister to Himself?

Answer: And this is central to the Good News, the Gospel of Jesus Christ, He walked this earthly trek as a man, not as God. In fact, his favorite name for Himself was the Son of Man. He had all the temptations and limitations of man, or in other words, as Adam and as you and me. Now we can walk as He did with our new powerful spirit because He lives in us. How else could He have instructed us to do the same, and greater things than He did, if He did them as God and not as a man? I am not divine or a god nor are you. We can't create a plant, a star, or even a grain of sand. We are mere men. However, He has given us the responsibility and the authority and the power to do what He did and even greater things when and if we will do what He told us to do:

> *If ye abide in me, and my words abide in you, ye shall ask what ye will, and it shall be done unto you. (John 15:7)*

We need to realize the angels ministered to the *man*, Christ Jesus, even as they can and will minister to us when we have the need.

> *Are they not all ministering spirits, sent forth to minister for them who shall be heirs of salvation? (Heb. 1:14)*

I want to tell you a real life story of ministering spirits at work. In March of 1995, I was driving from Omaha to Central City, Nebraska. It was a snowy day with wet slush on the roads, but I wasn't worried. I had a big 1983 full-sized Cadillac, and I was having no problem driving, until this instance. As you come into Central City there is a curve to the right. As I turned the steering wheel, nothing happened. I kept going straight! I looked up, and I was headed directly into a Buick with four people in it, and we were going to collide! I knew it and said, "Oh my word!" I closed my eyes and waited for the impact, which did not come.

When I opened my eyes, I saw my car was right where I expected it to be, in the left lane, where their car should have been, but wasn't! I looked in my side mirror, and they were fifty yards or more down the road. I turned my wheel, and it turned this time. I got back on my side of the road and was shaking. I knew that an angel had intervened to save all of us, and I praised the Lord all the way back to Omaha. Yes, angels are real, and they help us mortals when needed.

Have you ever considered the fact that Jesus could have failed? Oh yes! That was the whole point. The first Adam failed. The second Adam had to have the same option, but praise God, he didn't fail. Satan must have thought, *I defeated the first Adam. I can and will defeat the second.* Jesus defeated the devil at every turn, as a man, not as God. And now his victory has been credited to us! We are to walk on top of the devil and his works because of what Jesus did for us as a covenant *man*.

> *Ye are of God, little children, and have overcome them: because greater is he that is in you, than he that is in the world. (1 John 4:4)*

Our trip to the garden is going to show us a battle plan for standing against the devil and his demons and receiving the best God has to offer. I believe some of our readers will see the truth of the Gospel. Not a gospel, but rather the Gospel (Good News) of Jesus Christ as it was preached and practiced in the early church. Then and only then, you and I and all believers will again do the works of Jesus, and "even greater works," just as He said we would. Hallelujah!

Have you ever been discouraged, as I have, seeing the failure of the church today, whatever the denomination, regarding these greater works?

We now move ahead about three years. This is the last week of Jesus's earthly sojourn. Some absolutely, incredible events are about to take place. A fast-moving fulfillment of prophecy is going to occur as Jesus approaches his garden of decision, Gethsemane.

Let's set the stage. The world has seen the most miraculous ministry in its history although confined to the "pleasant land." Many believed, repented, and turned from their old wicked ways. Thousands of people have heard the words of life and countless healing, deliverance and miracles have taken place. Blind eyes have been opened, deaf ears heard, lame limbs walked, and people have even been raised from the dead. The apostle John wrote many years later still standing in awe.

> *And there are also many other things which Jesus did, the which, if they should be written every one, I suppose that even the world itself could not contain the books that should be written. Amen. (John 21:25)*

An idiom? Yes, but the point is clear, miracles, healing, feeding the multitudes, calming the sea, raising the dead had become everyday events, common place to Jesus's followers, which is the reason Jesus was so amazed at their continued lack of faith, especially the chosen twelve;

And immediately Jesus stretched forth his hand, and caught him, and said unto him, O thou of little faith, wherefore didst thou doubt? (Matt. 14:31)

The last week of Jesus's life was full to the brim, with one exception. He rested on the Sabbath. He healed blind Bartemaus plus two unnamed men in Jericho. He dined with Zacchaeus as he saw salvation enter his home. He walked toward Jerusalem, paused to order his chariot, an ass and her colt, and wept over the city of God's kings. "Oh, Jerusalem, Jerusalem!"

O Jerusalem, Jerusalem, thou that killest the prophets, and stonest them which are sent unto thee, how often would I have gathered thy children together, even as a hen gathereth her chickens under her wings, and ye would not! (Matt. 23:37)

We might ask is He saying the same thing about us today?

We who live in America need to take into account the great blessings that have been bestowed on us. The first is that we were born here. Only six percent of the earth's population lives in America. We had a 94 percent chance to not be born in America! Look at the blessing we have.

Whenever I start to complain about events in my life, I stop and remind myself of all these blessings. We do not live in a country that kills Christians or imprisons them or steals their possessions. We have available to us adequate food clothing and shelter. We should start each day and live each day praising God and glorifying Him. (Read my poem "Glorify" at the back at this book, which was given to me while in prison.)

Jesus entered the city as a conquering hero. "Hosanna to the highest," the people shouted. The same ones who will shout, "Crucify him!" before the week is over. He left the city as a vagabond to sleep in the hills.

He drove the merchants out of the temple area twice, shouting,

> *And said unto them, It is written, My house shall be called the house of prayer; but ye have made it a den of thieves. (Matt. 21:13)*

> *And he went into the temple, and began to cast out them that sold therein, and them that bought. (Luke 19:45)*

We see him curse a fig tree and in doing so taught his disciples a valuable lesson:

> *For verily I say unto you, That whosoever shall say unto this mountain, Be thou removed, and be thou cast into the sea; and shall not doubt in his heart, but shall believe that those things which he saith shall come to pass; he shall have whatsoever he saith.*

> *Therefore I say unto you, What things soever ye desire, when ye pray, believe that ye receive them, and ye shall have them.*

> *And when ye stand praying, forgive, if ye have ought against any: that your Father also which is in heaven may forgive you your trespasses.*

*But if ye do not forgive, neither will your Father
which is in heaven forgive your trespasses.*

(Mark 11:23–26)

In reality, this is the universal, God-given formula for success in any enterprise we attempt.

He was anointed twice in preparation for his burial, once by Mary, Lazarus's sister, and once in the home of Simon (once a leper before he met Jesus). The ointment in this anointing cost the equivalent of almost a year's salary! This anointing took place at suppers he attended this last week.

A third time he entered the temple area just to look around, perhaps to see if the "thieves" had returned. He taught daily in the temple this last week, except on the Sabbath. He continued to teach the people with parables.

Then in the Gospel of John, chapters 12–16, we have the most complete record of a discourse, which is worthy of our continued study for exhortation. The seventeenth chapter is Jesus's prayer to the Father for his disciples and for those who would believe "because of their words." That includes you and me!

There are two things of interest I would like to share with you.

First, in John 12:20 and 21, we see certain Gentiles, not Jews, not priests, not circumcised men, not Jesus's brethren, but the "dogs" ask Philip for an audience.

*And there were certain Greeks among them that
came up to worship at the feast:*

*The same came therefore to Philip, which was
of Bethsaida of Galilee, and desired him, saying,
"Sir, we would see Jesus." (John 12:20–21)*

Oh, that people today would come with that simple request, "We would see Jesus." Not we would see miracles or talking in tongues, but "We would see Jesus."

Our desire needs to be for the relationship and the fellowship of the Father, the promise giver, not for the promises. Remember the following:

> *But seek ye first the kingdom of God, and his righteousness; and all these things shall be added unto you. (Matt. 6:33)*

I believe the receipt of the promises is depended upon our acceptance of the Father without them. It is only with that kind of a pure heart that we can be trusted with them. This is another truth that God showed me through Nita, my wife. It is because she doesn't know it or see it herself that God have given her an extraordinary inner and outer beauty. God can and does trust her with this gift because Nita's eyes are on Jesus, not on herself.

Second, the prayer he prayed for himself, his disciples, and for us. Follow along in your Bible as we take a closer look at John, chapter 17.

Verses 1–5 are a revelation of Jesus's relationship with God his Father. Verses 6–10 are his report on his activities concerning his disciples. Verse 11 is a prophecy. Verses 12–19 are a continuing report in reference to the disciples. Verses 20–26 give us his prayer for all believers including you and me.

> *Neither pray I for these alone, but for them also which shall believe on me through their word;*

That they all may be one; as thou, Father, art in me, and I in thee, that they also may be one in us: that the world may believe that thou hast sent me.

And the glory which thou gavest me I have given them; that they may be one, even as we are one:

I in them, and thou in me, that they may be made perfect in one; and that the world may know that thou hast sent me, and hast loved them, as thou hast loved me.

Father, I will that they also, whom thou hast given me, be with me where I am; that they may behold my glory, which thou hast given me: for thou lovedst me before the foundation of the world.

O righteous Father, the world hath not known thee: but I have known thee, and these have known that thou hast sent me.

And I have declared unto them thy name, and will declare it: that the love wherewith thou hast loved me may be in them, and I in them. (John 17:20–26)

Jesus always received and, as our intercessor, still always receives answers to his prayers. I would suggest a time of intense meditation on this prayer and the personal application that it will engender. Perhaps you could use the following as a worship starter.

Father

From a distance the group of men looked no different than hundreds of others who had left the city to spend the night in the hills. The celebrants being more in number than the city's capacity to hold them, had to sleep wherever they could find space. The hills surrounding the city were covered with tents and booths for resting and sleeping; and outside, people were milling about the whole area, making it hard to move.

There were twelve men, walking slowly, listening intently to one who seemed to be their leader. They left the eastern gate of the city and followed the well-worn path down to the brook, pausing occasionally as the speaker made a point he wanted them to remember.

As we draw closer, we see the speaker is instructing more than conversing with his followers and there is a sense of urgency in his voice. As they approach the brook, the leader stops so suddenly that two of his men stumble over the ones in front of them. Then gathering themselves they stand waiting.

The moon had been the only light as they made their way through the night, and now it seemed to increase its brightness as the leader paused and looked toward heaven. His followers gathered around him in anticipation, thinking perhaps he had some special words to complete what he had been teaching them.

Just before he speaks, we too see his face shining in the moonlight and we are as entranced as his friends are. There is a brightness that is almost iridescent. It is awe inspiring as we see the face of one totally enraptured in what he is doing. His eyes are fastened on some distant place in the night sky. A look of longing spreads over his face slowly like a ripple on a pond and a smile forms as a tear winds its way from the corner of his eye, making a path down his cheek before dropping to his cloak. He opens his mouth and speaks in quiet reverence, in holy awe a word filled with a love and trust unknown to mankind until now.

> *In the beginning was the Word, and the Word was*
> *with God, and the Word was God. (John 1:1)*

Jesus calls out saying, "Father."

Here we have the Son of God on the precipice of great anguish and inexplicable pain both physical and mental, calling out, not crying out, but calling out to his Father in adoring, worshiping love!

Again, Jesus calls out saying, "Father."

We can see a smile of child-like trust as he looks up.

Again, Jesus calls out to his Father.

As a father, I remember the eyes of my children as they looked up to me and said, "Daddy." They trusted me to solve all their problems, heal all their hurts, remove all of life's obstacles; and they never questioned my ability to meet their needs and wants or my love.

My love for them was more than expected by them. It was more than believed to be there for them, it was lived in. They lived in the protection of, the deliverance of, and the warmth of my love. If someone were to have asked them then or even now though they are adults if their dad loves them, they would look dumbfounded.

"Well, of course, he does! How stupid to question whether Dad loves me! He has always loved me. I've never even wondered about that."

> *Ask, and it shall be given you; seek, and ye shall*
> *find; knock, and it shall be opened unto you:*
> *(Matt. 7:7)*

Love is definitely a good gift.

As Jesus says "Father," his word and attitude denote not only complete devotion, but also complete trust. I remember the trusting eyes of each of our children melting my heart, and I realize that God my Father loves me *more* than I love my children either when they were small or now.

So, should I trust my heavenly Father less than my children trusted me? I think not!

I believe this is the hardest thing for us to overcome in our relationship with God. Our traditions or denominational doctrines have taught us to fear God, to doubt him and his power or goodness, and to blame him for tragedies. Then they tell us that he loves us and we should love him.

Tell a parent who has just lost a child or a widow who just lost her husband that God in his love took their loved one because he, God, needed him or her more than they did (now that's neurotic or just plain stupid). But they are to love him anyway and believe that he loves them! How can we expect people to trust a God who "steals" their joy?

We accept in religion, ideas that are so illogical, that we would immediately reject them in any other relationship. In fact, if our God is responsible for the acts we accuse him of, we could put him in prison. And we should!

Our God is love. Love doesn't hate!

Our God is life. Life doesn't kill!

Our God is merciful. Mercy doesn't torture!

Our God pities us. He doesn't prey on us!

We need to have the attitude of Jesus when we go to our Father the attitude of saying.

"Father I trust you completely. I love you fully. I believe you without any doubt. I commend myself, spirit, soul, and body to you and your keeping. Right now, Father, I fall into you, knowing that your arms are stretched out ready to catch me and to hold me safely in your care."

Father.

Questions:

1. Have I learned and taught my children the promised benefits of obedience to parents especially to our Heavenly Father?
2. Is the principle of blessing for obedience to God in my mind and heart?
3. Have I learned that obedience to God's plan for my life may not seem right or logical to me? Yet I trust that he knows what is best for me.

Activity:

Begin today to personalize the Scriptures. Instead of reading the Psalm 91 as "He who dwells…," read, "I dwell…"

CHAPTER 3

A MAN NAMED JOSHUA

To better understand the times, let us step into the life of Joshua, a man of that time. He, like all of Israel, is waiting for the Messiah. Although not a priest, he is a scribe and he knows the law and the prophets and feels that the time of the Messiah's arrival is at hand.

Joshua is of the same generation as Jesus although a few years older and therefore escaped the slaughter of the innocents some thirty plus years before. Joshua's name was even the same as Jesus's. *Jesus* being the Greek translation of the Hebrew *Joshua*, and it means, "God with us." Many women in Israel named their sons Joshua hoping that perhaps their son was the Messiah.

Joshua had watched the ministry of this itinerant preacher first with skepticism, then curiosity, then hope and, finally, belief. But then I am getting ahead of myself.

*   *   *

Joshua recalled the first time he had encountered Jesus of Nazareth. It was about three years ago at Passover, and Jesus had cause a terrible scene and subsequent problems. Thousands of people from all over Jewry were in Jerusalem to observe these most important and holy of feasts, the Passover, followed by the Feast of Unleavened Bread. God ordered Moses to initiate Passover on the fourteenth day of the first month, Abib. The Feast of Unleavened Bread began on the fifteenth day with a special Sabbath and continued for seven days with the last day being a special Sabbath as well.

As an example, if the fourteenth day of Abib, Passover, fell on a Wednesday, the fifteenth, Thursday, would be the special Sabbath. Then the regular Sabbath would fall on Saturday with the last day of the feast, Wednesday the twenty-first, being again a special Sabbath. This is very important as we will see later.

Some estimates are that over five hundred thousand people would be in Jerusalem for these yearly feasts. Add to this number the residents of the city and it is easy to see that it would not be unusual for over 250,000 animals to be sacrificed during these feasts. In case you are not familiar with the law and practice at that time, here it is: the animals were sacrificed, the blood was shed on the altar, but the carcasses were given back to the people to consume at the Passover feast.

That Passover three years ago was normal for attendance, but what was unusual was the entrance of the preacher Jesus. He walked into the temple area where the licensed merchants sold animals to be sacrificed to the out-of-towners and overturned their tables. Then using a whip he made of some cords, he drove the merchants and the animals from the temple. He opened the dove's cages and let them go free. It took several days and an extraordinary effort on the part of the merchants and the priests to round up the scattered animals in time for the sacrifices.

But what Joshua remembered more than that and what was burned into his memory was the picture of this itinerant preacher standing on one of the tables, shouting with a voice filled with a fierceness and zeal never heard before: "Take these things hence and make not my Father's house a house of merchandise!"

A group of Joshua's colleges had responded to the action in anger and rebuke, asking Jesus to show them a sign or a miracle to prove that he had the right or God's blessing to do these things. After all, what right did he have to disrupt their way of worship?

Jesus answered them, "Destroy this temple, and in three days I will raise it up again."

Jesus then turned his back on the religious leaders and began to teach the people, and he performed so many miracles of healing that the priests were afraid to say anything against him for fear of the people. Many of the people who were healed or who saw the healing believed that he was the Messiah. However, when Jesus was asked directly, he would neither confirm nor deny. Joshua took all these happenings in with tremendous interest and determined he would research the Scriptures for all references to the Messiah. Then just as suddenly as Jesus had appeared on the religious scene in Jerusalem, he disappeared.

As soon as the feast days were completed that year, Joshua asked for a private conference with Joseph of Arimathea, one of the most prestigious members of the Sanhedrin, a Pharisee, and a man anxiously awaiting the arrival of the Messiah. When Joshua explained what he wanted to discuss, Joseph suggested they include his good friend Nicodemus because of his contact with Jesus.

They met the day after the feast celebrations, while everyone was busy either leaving for home, helping friends and family prepare to leave, or helping to clean up the messes and the rearrangement caused by the visitors.

Joshua had a great deal of respect for these two men. They weren't like so many of Israel's leaders who were political, ambitious, and greedy. He knew they were godly men, and he also felt they knew things about this Jesus that he didn't know and that they didn't talk about. He had heard them say quietly that they believed that the Messiah was alive right now and would soon show himself to Israel.

Joshua had listened with surface interest in the past; but with the arrival of and the activities of this itinerant preacher Jesus, well, Joshua wanted to hear all they knew and what they speculated.

Joseph and Joshua had been exchanging pleasantries for just a few minutes when Nicodemus arrived. He greeted them and sat down.

Joseph spoke first. "Nicodemus, my good friend, how good of you to join us. Joshua has asked me to share the benefit of our years and research into the arrival of the Messiah. I knew you had spoken to the young preacher from Galilee, Jesus, the other night so I wanted you to be here. I think we should start at the beginning, don't you?"

Nicodemus nodded, then looked at Joseph with a question mark on his face.

Joseph understood, and to quiet his friend's fears, he said, "I believe Joshua is an honorable man and can be trusted to be discreet at least until we are sure who this Jesus is."

Nicodemus nodded again He studied Joshua's face, searching his eyes as if to assure himself that Joshua was as sincere as he seemed to be. It was only prudent, in this day and age, with all the innuendoes and broken confidences to be sure of the reasons for such an inquiry. Satisfied, he began.

"Joshua, you were just a child, but I'm sure you have heard the stories, perhaps you've even read some of our official reports, our written account, of the child born to the priest Zachariah and his wife Elizabeth of Judea. What made this birth so special were first the advanced age of the parents and the visit. In fact, we saw a real comparison to the birth of Isaac to Abraham and Sarah. Oh, the excitement. After over four hundred years of silence, the Lord God was speaking to us again.

"Not everyone felt that way, though, most of the leaders thought Zachariah had lost his mind. In fact, someone even suggested that maybe Elizabeth had committed…"

His voice trailed off as he said almost under his breath, "Why do we always want to believe the worst and doubt the sovereignty of God?

"After the birth of the child, Zachariah related to us of the visit he had from the angel Gabriel and the announcement that this child would fulfill the prophecy of Isaiah that he spoke concerning looking beyond the captivity as

> *'The voice of him that crieth in the wilderness,*
> *Prepare ye the way of the LORD, make straight in*
> *the desert a highway for our God' (Isa. 40:3).*

The angel gave instructions on how the child should be raised.

> *'For he shall be great in the sight of the Lord, and*
> *shall drink neither wine nor strong drink; and he*
> *shall be filled with the Holy Ghost, even from his*
> *mother's womb' (Luke 1:15)."*

Nicodemus paused, allowing Joshua to assimilate this information before going on. When he felt Joshua was ready, he continued.

"This occurred a little over thirty years ago, Joshua, when Joseph and I were about your age. We were so excited. We wanted to tell everyone, but when we tried, most people just laughed. That's why even though we've been expecting the Messiah, we do our seeking quietly. It did not surprise us when the old man Simeon who spent his days, after his wife died in the temple worshipping and praising God told us shortly after the taxing ordered by Caesar Augustus that a child was brought into the temple to be presented to the Lord as directed by Moses being the firstborn son of a peasant couple from Nazareth. This occurred about six months after Zachariah's son was born.

"Simeon took us aside after the couple had left the Temple and said, 'Now I can die in peace. Our God has let me see the salvation of the Lord. For the Holy Spirit had revealed to me that I would not see death until I had seen his Christ. He, God's own son, was just presented to the priests for dedication according to the Law of Moses. God in his mercy has brought the child into the Temple while I was here. Then he confirmed that this was indeed his son by Anna.'

"Now Anna was an old woman who lived here in the Temple, spending all her days as an instrument of God's praise. She seeing the child began to speak to all who were near telling how God's deliverance had arrived. When I heard the announcement from Simeon, I ran outside in hopes of seeing the baby but I was too late. They had already been swallowed up in the crowd."

Again, Nicodemus paused, but this time it was for his own benefit. He needed to take a few moments to for perhaps the thousandth time dispel the feeling that "if only I had seen the child as they did, perhaps my faith…"

He went on speaking.

"It was about two years later, maybe a little less that one of the most horrible, despicable acts ever committed by any human being was committed by King Herod, son of Antipater."

Joseph snorted, "King? Ha! He wasn't even a Jew and neither are his sons!"

Nicodemus continued, "There were 'seers,' wise men from the east, Persia, I think, who came and presented themselves to him to inquire of the whereabouts of the 'king' born to rule the Jews. They claimed they had followed a heavenly sign a bright star to the land of the Jews and that it was a prophesied omen announcing his birth. When the king heard this, he was troubled and all Jerusalem with him. The king sent for the chief priest and the scribes and asked about the prophecies concerning the birth of the Lord's Christ. He was told in Bethlehem of Judah.

> *But thou, Bethlehem Ephratah, though thou be little among the thousands of Judah, yet out of thee shall he come forth unto me that is to be ruler in Israel; whose goings forth have been from of old, from everlasting. (Mic. 5:2)*

"King Herod told the visitors of the Bethlehem prophecy and then instructed them to report back to him after they found the child so he, the king, could also come and worship him. Some of us suspected that Herod had other reasons for wanting to know the child's whereabouts, and unfortunately, we were right to be concerned.

"The men from the East never returned to see the king, and Herod was so incensed that he ordered the murder of every male child two years old and younger in the whole region. Thus was the prophecy of Jeremiah fulfilled."

> *Thus saith the LORD; A voice was heard in Ramah, lamentation, and bitter weeping; Rachel weeping for her children refused to be comforted for her children, because they were not. (Jer. 31:15)*

Nicodemus stood up, walked a bit. His shoulders shook as he shuddered remembering the time and his second son. One never forgets the loss of a child. He returned to his seat and continued.

"We lost track of the child and the parents until a Passover Feast about ten years later. There was nothing special about this feast. We were so busy with what seemed like an extra number of worshippers, and then on the day everyone was going home, a lad entered the temple and began to discuss the Law of Moses with the doctors of the law and with wisdom far beyond his years. He stayed here with the priests and debated, discussed, and questioned them for three days until his parents came to take him home.

"I was there the day they came to get him and marveled at his wisdom. I was about to ask if he was the Messiah when his parents arrived. They both looked so tired but relieved, but it was his mother who asked, scolding him, 'Son why have you dealt with us so?' Joshua, his answer caught us all off guard. I did not want to forget his exact words, so I wrote them down."

Fumbling a bit, he finally produced an aged paper and read, "Did you not know I must be about my Father's business?

"Once again before I could question him, he was gone. Remembering what the king's father had done when he felt his authority threatened, we decided we would not mention our suspicions to anyone outside of the temple."

At this point Nicodemus paused and seemed somewhat reluctant to speak further, so Joseph picked up the discourse.

"Nicodemus and I have calculated that if he was, and is, the Christ, then this is his thirtieth year. And as you know, according to the rules of the elders, he should make himself known. The Messiah should reveal himself in his thirtieth year!"

Joseph stopped to draw a deep breath in a way to make his listeners expect a revelation, then said, "Then here comes this preacher Jesus. What does he do? He cleans out the temple, chasing the merchants. He calls the temple his Father's house. He preaches, saying the kingdom of God has come. He heals the sick, and he is doing all the things the Messiah was prophesied to do."

*And the Jews' passover was at hand, and Jesus went
up to Jerusalem,*

And found in the temple those that sold oxen and sheep and doves, and the changers of money sitting:

And when he had made a scourge of small cords, he drove them all out of the temple, and the sheep, and the oxen; and poured out the changers' money, and overthrew the tables;

And said unto them that sold doves, Take these things hence; make not my Father's house an house of merchandise.

And his disciples remembered that it was written, The zeal of thine house hath eaten me up. (John 2:13–17)

Nicodemus broke in, "We know he is of God, but is he the Messiah?" The tone of his voice betrayed the great struggle of this godly man.

"Nicodemus." It was Joseph again. "Tell Joshua of your meeting with Jesus."

By now Joshua was so consumed by the story, so rapt in attention, he hadn't noticed that others had gathered around the elders to listen in. But this added attention was making Nicodemus and Joseph quite nervous. Nicodemus paused in his narrative to scan the crowd. Satisfied that the listeners were of the younger set and not members of what he called the "keepers of tradition," he continued.

"After Jesus's actions and comments concerning the merchants and his teachings and miracles in the Temple, I talked to Joseph and some of the other council members and we decided one of us should try to meet with Jesus to question him privately and to ask him if in fact he is the Messiah. I volunteered. I found him in his favorite resting place, a garden on the lower part of the Mount of Olivet's, called Gethsemane on the other side on the brook Kidron. When we met, he invited me to sit with him and I wasted no time. I really wanted to know was he or wasn't he the Messiah?

> *There was a man of the Pharisees, named Nicodemus, a ruler of the Jews:*
>
> *The same came to Jesus by night, and said unto him, Rabbi, we know that thou art a teacher come from God: for no man can do these miracles that thou doest, except God be with him.*
>
> *Jesus answered and said unto him, Verily, verily, I say unto thee, except a man be born again, he cannot see the kingdom of God. (John 3:1–3)*

"Joshua, I've searched the Scriptures diligently. I believe that Jesus of Nazareth is truly the Messiah, the Son of God!"

Joseph nodded. "So do I." Then he added, "But what do we do now? Is God expecting us to herald his coming? If so, why hasn't God spoken to us or why hasn't Jesus said something? What if we are to remain silent for now to allow God's plan to come to fruition? How can we be sure of anything?"

Nicodemus said, "I am going to meet Him again this very night."

*   *   *

Nicodemus rose from supper and said to his wife, "I have heard that Jesus spends time in Joseph's garden on the other side of the brook Kidron. I must speak to him again before he leaves the city. I must know who he is. You know how much I care for Israel and our faith, our traditions. I will not compromise my beliefs, I will not be moved by teachings that offend the elders, but I must talk to him again. I must know absolutely who he is. I'm going to walk up there tonight. I must see Jesus."

She too had heard much of Jesus and his ministry and was anxious to hear what he would say to her husband. "Be careful, Nicodemus, and tell me everything when you return."

A kiss on the check and Nicodemus left on his mission. Quite frankly, he didn't want anyone to know about this meeting any more than the first one, but he must know who Jesus was and if he really was the Messiah, Galilee or no Galilee!

On the way to the meeting, the thought kept going through his mind, *I care about our traditions! I care about appearances! I care! Doesn't Jesus care?*

The Prophecy
Six Days before Passover

> *Then many of the Jews which came to Mary, and had seen the things which Jesus did, believed on him.*

> *But some of them went their ways to the Pharisees, and told them what things Jesus had done.*

> *Then gathered the chief priests and the Pharisees a council, and said, What do we? for this man doeth many miracles.*

If we let him thus alone, all men will believe on him: and the Romans shall come and take away both our place and nation.

And one of them, named Caiaphas, being the high priest that same year, said unto them, Ye know nothing at all,

Nor consider that it is expedient for us, that one man should die for the people, and that the whole nation perish not.

And this spake he not of himself: but being high priest that year, he prophesied that Jesus should die for that nation;

And not for that nation only, but that also he should gather together in one the children of God that were scattered abroad. (John 11:45–52)

It now was three years later and another Passover feast, and Jesus had returned. He had been in Jerusalem at last year's Passover, had taught and healed the people, but as before, he had left the city to preach in the outlying countryside. But this year was different. Joshua had spent every free minute he had searching the scriptures for himself, and he found two references that convinced him that this preacher, Jesus, was indeed God's own anointed, the very Christ, and that he, Joshua, was watching history in the making as the Lord God must be ready to place Jesus, his Son, on the throne of David, his rightful place as Isaiah the prophet wrote so many years before.

The Spirit of the Lord GOD is upon me; because the LORD hath anointed me to preach good tidings unto the meek; he hath sent me to bind up the brokenhearted, to proclaim liberty to the captives, and the opening of the prison to them that are bound;

To proclaim the acceptable year of the LORD, and the day of vengeance of our God; to comfort all that mourn;

To appoint unto them that mourn in Zion, to give unto them beauty for ashes, the oil of joy for mourning, the garment of praise for the spirit of heaviness; that they might be called trees of righteousness, the planting of the LORD, that he might be glorified.

And they shall build the old wastes, they shall raise up the former desolations, and they shall repair the waste cities, the desolations of many generations.

And strangers shall stand and feed your flocks, and the sons of the alien shall be your plowmen and your vinedressers.

But ye shall be named the Priests of the LORD: men shall call you the Ministers of our God: ye shall eat the riches of the Gentiles, and in their glory shall ye boast yourselves. (Isa. 61:1-6)

He especially liked the last part of the prophecy. He, Joshua, would eat the riches of these pagan Roman gentiles and would serve in the Messiah's administration. He knew he would! If only he could meet Jesus. He was sure He would see that he had the talent to be of great value to Him in the new Kingdom. Then the clincher.

Rejoice greatly, O daughter of Zion; shout, O daughter of Jerusalem: behold, thy King cometh unto thee: he is just, and having salvation; lowly, and riding upon an ass, and upon a colt the foal of an ass. (Zech. 9:9)

Jesus had done just that two days ago, and now he was going to do it again.

The Council Meets
Sunday before the Passover

Then assembled together the chief priests, and the scribes, and the elders of the people, unto the palace of the high priest, who was called Caiaphas,

And consulted that they might take Jesus by subtilty, and kill him.

But they said, Not on the feast day, lest there be an uproar among the people. (Matt. 26:3–5)

Caiaphas looked around to see if everyone, all *seventy* members, were present for this meeting. Although the law allowed the Sanhedrin to meet and make decisions with only a simple majority attending, this was too important an issue to address for even one member to be absent.

While he waited for the last two stragglers to arrive, amid the din of conversation of those already there, Caiaphas reflected on the reason for his unusual concern over this meeting. The Sanhedrin met every day of the week, with the exception of Sabbaths and holy days, but this meeting would be different due to "the problem"!

As high priest, it was his responsibility to protect the faith of Israel. Anyone who challenged the authority of the faith, the Torah, the Talmud, or the high priest (this year that was him) would feel the wrath of his power and the power of the Sanhedrin. He'd see to that. He recalled that rebel from Galilee, Judas, who rose up in the days of the census, and before him there was Theudas. Each time their followers proclaimed them to be the savior of Israel, and each time the Sanhedrin, the council of the elders, had to explain to the king and to the Roman procurator that they had nothing to do with these rebels. In fact, Israel and its rulers had not had such peace and prosperity at any time in their history as they had now under the "protection" or occupation of Rome. Now this new fellow was creating problems with the people.

Caiaphas's concentration was broken when his father-in-law Annas said, "Everyone is here, Caiaphas, you can begin."

Caiaphas looked over the council, the greatest men in Jehovah's Israel, the judges, and only within the past twenty-five years had their authority been what it should have been all along. It was ironic that it took the Roman occupation to bring about the true power of the Sanhedrin. They now had the legal right to rule all of Israel, and as the oldest and wisest of men, they deserved that right.

Well, he thought, *this august assembly, God's chosen men for this time in our nation's history certainly will go down in the history of our people as the finest most righteous of all generations. We are zealous of our faith, our beliefs.*

He looked at the men and took count. There was Annas, his father-in-law, and the high priest last year to his right. Annas had seen five of his sons ascend to the office of High Priest, and now he, his son-inlaw. Surely this great man of God will be highly honored by God and the Messiah in His kingdom one day!

Next to Annas sat his sons, then Gamaliel, the most highly revered teacher of the law in all of Israel and behind him sat his most learned and zealous student, Saul of Tarsus, who no doubt would one day be a member. Nicodemus was seated next to and was conversing with Joseph of Arimathea, his good friend, and one who believed the Messiah's coming was imminent.

There was John and Alexander and Jarius and so many others he counted as friends and some not, some whose opinions he respected and some he only tolerated, some were Pharisees, some Sadducees, and some Zealots. Caiaphas tried to keep himself above the fray of their political infighting as he believed it was necessary to assure the continuance of the free exercise of their religion during the Roman occupation. Just the other day he had an audience with King Herod, and there seemed to be agreement that the preservation of Israel depended upon calm and clear heads in a time of national expectancy of deliverance by the Messiah and the reality of the rule of Rome. Herod was not his idea of a king of Israel, but Rome had appointed him, and Israel had to live with that situation, as well as the tyranny of Rome.

"Fathers of Israel, I've called you together to discuss a problem brewing in our nation. It's the Jesus problem!

"We had that baptizer, John, preaching repentance toward God, which was a positive message, but then he started condemning us, Israel's leaders. As you recall we sent some of you, priests and Levities, to question him, and he claimed he was not the Messiah, but was the one to announce His coming.

"Now, I can accept God choosing our generation to bring forth his anointed in fact, I hope he does. I for one would gladly welcome him, give him the honor he deserves. I would gladly give him my seat on the council, but we have the responsibility to keep the way clear of impostors and I, as I'm sure you have as well, checked the Scriptures. The Messiah does not come from Galilee, where this Jesus hails from, so it certainly would seem he is just another pretender to the throne of David.

"The question remains then, who is this Jesus and who gives him the right to take authority over our merchants who provide such a valuable service to our worshipers, especially those from distant areas? We all know that we have allowed this free exercise of trade as a convenience for them. There is no need for me to bring up the profitability for our members. After all we all share in the fees charged the merchants, and this practice has been approved by the Sanhedrin.

"Jesus was in the temple area, chasing them out the day before the Sabbath, and this created havoc for our people and upset the merchants and all this as we prepare for the Passover two days hence. I would like some thoughts and information from those of you who have met or seen him."

One of the younger members spoke up and related that he and a few of his friends had been in the area when Jesus committed this act and they had confronted him. "I asked him what sign he would show us as to his authority to do these things. I like all of you have heard the rumors of miracles he has performed in Capernaum, as well as in all the cities around us, and gave him an opportunity to display his powers if he has any. And he said to me, 'Destroy this temple, and in three days I will raise it up.' We laughed, and I said, 'It has taken forty-six years to build this temple, and will you raise it up in three days?'"

There was a short silence, then Joseph said, "No man can heal the sick like he can, unless God is with him."

Nicodemus agreed with him and asked, "Does not our own law require that we examine a man and let him answer for himself before we condemn him?"

One after another of the members spoke their minds with no clear resolution except to have some of their more learned ones question him as opportunities presented themselves. Righteous indignation abounded as the zeal of defending the "faith" of Israel caused even some of the more docile ones to vent their frustrations.

Then before a vote could be taken, although Caiaphas saw the majority of the members were in agreement with him that the Jesus problem needed resolution, a disciple of the Pharisees came running into the court shouting, "He's doing it again!"

As one, the members turned and ran to the temple to confront this impostor.

As they arrived, they say the deed was done and Jesus was speaking to the merchants:

> *Saying unto them, It is written, My house is the house of prayer: but ye have made it a den of thieves. (Luke 19:46)*

They would have taken him then, as angry as they were, but the people were attentive and believed in him. So, for fear of the people, the leaders turned away and determined to wait until after the Feast of Unleavened Bread, as many had believed on him after seeing the miracles he had performed.

As Jesus turned to leave, his eyes and Nicodemus's met and Nicodemus purposed in his heart to see Jesus that night if h e could find him. There was something about this man that was so different he must investigate personally.

The meeting was over, as was the confrontation, but not the conversation. Everyone had an opinion and wanted to express it to anyone who would listen.

As Caiaphas was leaving, he said to no one in particular, "This Jesus problem is not going to go away until he goes away or someone kills him. We do have the responsibility to protect our nation. Better he die than us. There must be a way."

Joshua could not remember a time he had ever been this excited before! He was, as his wife had said, beside himself. The Prophet, the Messiah, Jesus of Nazareth, was coming to Jerusalem riding on the foal of an ass. Glory be! This was it. He had lived to see the Messiah arrive to take his rightful place on the throne of David. May the Lord God be praised. He tripped and stumbled as he ran to meet him. "I must meet him today!"

There had been a spontaneous celebration the day before the Sabbath when Jesus came into Jerusalem riding on a colt with the crowds running along with him, shouting, "Hosanna to the son of David" and had strewn the path with branches and coats. He, Joshua, had missed it although he had been in the temple when the throngs of people following Jesus filled every court of the temple trying to be near him. They were shouting, "Hosanna in the highest," and, glorifying God, had converged on the Temple. And it appeared for a time like the people were ready to take him by force and make him king in the place of Herod.

The whole city was stirred by his appearance, with many asking, "Who is this?" And his followers were shouting, "This is Jesus, the prophet from Nazareth of Galilee."

The people thought Jesus had stopped at the temple to announce to the priests that he was indeed the Messiah, then go on to the palace. But instead he took a rope and started whipping the merchants selling animals and the money changers, chasing them out of the temple! Then there was a heated exchange of charges and countercharges between Jesus and the scribes and Pharisees. Then just as suddenly as he had arrived, he left, not to take the throne but to leave town.

Joshua heard the murmuring of the crowd, expressing their disappointment, and the murmurs became louder until they who had shouted hosanna were shouting questions. "Are you the one who was to come or should we look for another?"

Jesus had not done what everyone expected him to do. He didn't take over the government!

Now on the first day of the week Jesus was back, and we had a repeat of the earlier trip. This time, however, everyone was sure that Jesus would do what was right and prophesied and take the throne. "We will have our king," was the shout of the people. He would take over the kingdom.

Joshua was convinced that Jesus was the Messiah, and he had every intention to be one of the first to stand with him. The crowd was pushing and shoving. The air was stifling, and it was with great difficulty that Joshua got close enough to even see Jesus let alone talk to him. But as the crowd from Jerusalem merged with the one coming with and surrounding Jesus as he rode into the city, somehow he found himself pushed and squeezed until suddenly he was beside the colt. His hand touched Jesus's cloak.

Joshua, startled at his good fortune, looked up into the face of Jesus just as Jesus turned to look at him. For the shortest of moments their eyes met, and Jesus smiled. All Joshua could see was love.

Joshua opened his mouth to speak, "You are the Messiah, aren't you?" But before he finished asking the question, the swirling crowd had moved him away and it was all he could do just to keep his feet.

The trip to Jerusalem, the stop at the temple, the words spoken all seemed to be a repeat of the last time. But surely this time he will take the throne. Surely this time!

But, no, he was leaving town again and the people were angry. This was too much. As he left the eastern gate, Joshua heard someone shout, "You're not the Messiah! You're a phony like all the rest! You didn't do what we wanted you to do what you're supposed to do. How can we believe in you?"

Questions:

1. Is God's will for my life more important to me than mine?
2. Have I been justifying my disobedience to God's will for me?
3. Have I learned that obedience to God's plan for my life may not seem right or logical to me?
4. Have I called Jesus or faith in God phony because I didn't get what I wanted when I wanted it? Have I repented?

Activity:

Begin today to seek Gods will for your life instead of your own.

CHAPTER 4

GOOD FRIDAY?

Even as a child I had a problem with Good Friday, so blame it on my German heritage. I like everything in rows, in lines, and to be correctly stated. I don't like inconsistencies. Here's the problem.

> *For as Jonas was three days and three nights in the*
> *whale's belly; so shall the Son of man be three days*
> *and three nights in the heart of the earth. (Matt.*
> *12:40)*

If Jesus said He would be in the heart of the earth for three days and three nights and if Jesus was crucified on Friday, we have a problem with a Sunday resurrection.

The fact of the matter is He was crucified on Wednesday, on Passover, the day before the Sabbath spoken of in John 19:31:

> *The Jews therefore, because it was the preparation,*
> *that the bodies should not remain upon the cross*
> *on the Sabbath day, (for that Sabbath day was an*
> *high day,) besought Pilate that their legs might be*
> *broken, and that they might be taken away.*

This was not the regular weekly Sabbath, but rather the first high day of the Feast of Unleavened Bread, which was celebrated for seven days beginning one day after the Passover, on the fifteenth of Abib, and ended with an additional high day, or special Sabbath, seven days later. The visitors to the tomb showed up on Sunday, the first day of the week.

It was important that Jesus's body be in the tomb for three days and nights, not only to fulfill His words, but also because the Jews believed a man's spirit stayed with the body for those three days and then it left, as the body began to decay. If he had arisen before the full three days had elapsed the Jews would have claimed that he hadn't really died, that his spirit had reentered his body. Remember the words of Lazarus's sister, Martha, as Jesus was about to raise him from the dead?

> *Jesus said, Take ye away the stone. Martha, the sister of him that was dead, saith unto him, Lord, by this time he stinketh: for he hath been dead four days. (John 11:39)*

So this was the special Sabbath commanded in Leviticus chapter 23, not the regular weekly Sabbath, and this is very important because of the timeline. God is a God of exactness. Everything he does and has done is very precise, just ask any scientist. Jesus had to die at the hour and day of the sacrifice of the lamb of Passover, and remember, He did. He gave up the ghost at the ninth hour, or three o'clock in the afternoon, and that was the hour of the sacrifice. He was buried before sunset so as not to defile the special Sabbath.

The Jewish day began and ended at sunset, as ours does at midnight. Jesus was in the "heart of the earth" Wednesday, Thursday, and Friday nights, and Thursday, Friday, and Saturday (the regular weekly Sabbath) days. Then His resurrection occurred after sunset on Saturday, the first day of their week, or what we call Sunday.

I believe one of the reasons the unbelieving world makes such fun of the Christian faith is that we Christians cling to traditions as if they were the Word of God and have ignored the simplicity of the Gospel. Jesus said of the religious leaders of His day.

> *And honour not his father or his mother, he shall*
> *be free. Thus have ye made the commandment of*
> *God of none effect by your tradition. (Matt. 15:6)*

We should celebrate Good Wednesday, and honor Christ's suffering through to glorious Sunday, but then we could not have a three-day weekend for fun and games, could we?

The Last Twenty-Four Hours

Now let's live the last twenty-four hours of Jesus's life on earth as a un-resurrected man, just as He did.

It's Tuesday sunset, the start of Wednesday, the day of the Passover sacrifice; and Jesus says to His disciples:

> *And he said unto them, With desire I have desired*
> *to eat this Passover with you before I suffer: (Luke*
> *22:15)*

We have no record of Jesus eating any other Passover with His disciples. In fact the law read that they were to eat it with their family. So what was this Passover/Last Supper all about? It seems that Jesus had let them know that He wanted to eat with them a day early, because of the following:

And he sent Peter and John, saying, Go and pre-
pare us the Passover, that we may eat. (Luke 22:8)

Now let's read on and we will find answers to what may have been perplexing questions to us in the past.

And they said unto him, Where wilt thou that we
prepare?

And he said unto them, Behold, when ye are
entered into the city, there shall a man meet you,
bearing a pitcher of water; follow him into the
house where he entereth in.

And ye shall say unto the good man of the house,
The Master saith unto thee, Where is the guest
chamber, where I shall eat the Passover with my
disciples?

And he shall shew you a large upper room fur-
nished: there make ready.

And they went, and found as he had said unto
them: and they made ready the Passover. (Luke
22:9–13)

Question:

Why would they notice this particular man? There would be thousands of men and women in the city, how would they know which was the right one?

Answer:

Women carried the jugs on their heads, not men, so if they saw a man with a water jug on his head they would notice!

Question:

With as many as five hundred thousand travelers in Jerusalem for the feast, besides the city inhabitants, what was the possibility of finding an available guest chamber for this supper?

Answer:

The sacrifice would not be killed until 3:00 p.m. the next day so although the room would be ready, it would normally not be used until the next evening. There were exceptions allowed due to personal difficulties, plus surely the author of the feast could eat it whenever he chose.

He broke the bread and shared it with them at the start of the meal and said the following:

> And he took bread, and gave thanks, and brake
> it, and gave unto them, saying, This is my body
> which is given for you: this do in remembrance of
> me. (Luke 22:19)

We have a pause here for the time to eat.
What was the conversation of the disciples?

> And there was also a strife among them, which
> of them should be accounted the greatest. (Luke
> 22:24)

He is speaking of sacrificing Himself for their salvation. They are arguing about who will be greatest in the new administration.

They still don't get it, do they? If I had been Jesus I would have been so angry and hurt to think that my friends were in strife and envy while I was in pain and torment knowing the things that are about to occur, that I'd have fired the whole bunch.

But then I'm not Jesus, Mr. Love Himself. Were they still expecting Jesus to take over the reins of government now?

I can almost hear them "Tomorrow has to be it! What a perfect day to start the messianic kingdom, the high Holy day of the feast. I'm willing to allow Jesus to give me the job (ministry) He wants me to have. I'm not going to ask for anything particular like John and James did. I'll be satisfied with His choice. But I wish He'd hurry up. I want to go home and tell my wife the good news. I mean if he could feed five thousand men plus women and children with a little boy's lunch, he will supply all we'll ever need."

I have meditated on this scripture many times when I had to "find" a way out of my difficulties, only when I trusted God did he give me the best way.

Maybe you don't think these "holy" men would even think, much less say such things, but I think they did. Why? Because you and I do all the time! We are always telling the Lord what to do and when to do it while we act so humble and holy! Don't we? Or is it just me?

Then Jesus does three extraordinary things. First, He institutes the second part of the Last Supper.

> *Likewise also the cup after supper, saying, This cup is the new testament in my blood, which is shed for you. (Luke 22:20)*

Second, He takes the position of the lowest slave in a household by washing their feet, to give an example of living a life of service both to Him and to each other.

He riseth from supper, and laid aside his garments; and took a towel, and girded himself.

After that he poureth water into a bason, and began to wash the disciples' feet, and to wipe them with the towel wherewith he was girded.

Then cometh he to Simon Peter: and Peter saith unto him, Lord, dost thou wash my feet?

Jesus answered and said unto him, What I do thou knowest not now; but thou shalt know hereafter.

Peter saith unto him, Thou shalt never wash my feet. Jesus answered him, If I wash thee not, thou hast no part with me.

Simon Peter saith unto him, Lord, not my feet only, but also my hands and my head.

Jesus saith to him, He that is washed needeth not save to wash his feet, but is clean every whit: and ye are clean, but not all.

For he knew who should betray him; therefore said he, Ye are not all clean.

So after he had washed their feet, and had taken his garments, and was set down again, he said unto them, Know ye what I have done to you?

Ye call me Master and Lord: and ye say well; for so I am.

If I then, your Lord and Master, have washed your feet; ye also ought to wash one another's feet.

For I have given you an example, that ye should do as I have done to you. (John 13:4–15)

And third, He names His betrayer. But let's read this account in John's Gospel. There is something we need to see.

And as they sat and did eat, Jesus said, Verily I say unto you, One of you which eateth with me shall betray me.

And they began to be sorrowful, and to say unto him one by one, Is it I? and another said, Is it I?

And he answered and said unto them, It is one of the twelve, that dippeth with me in the dish. (Mark 14:18–20)

These great men of faith, the ones to whom Jesus will entrust the propagation of the Gospel want to know if they are going to betray Him. This lets me know there is hope for me. Don't despair if you stumble or fail at times, just run to Jesus and bury yourself in His love.

Then we see him naming his betrayer, yet except for Judas, no one seemed to have grasped it.

And after the sop Satan entered into him. Then said Jesus unto him, That thou doest, do quickly.

Now no man at the table knew for what intent he spake this unto him.

For some of them thought, because Judas had the bag, that Jesus had said unto him, Buy those things that we have need of against the feast; or, that he should give something to the poor. (John 13:27–29)

Did they think that they would celebrate their feast again on the morrow? Or that he should give something to the poor.

Then he continues to institutes the Lord's Supper or communion by sharing the wine and the bread. We in the Western world have difficulty understanding covenants, especially blood covenants. A covenant is a contract, and in America, our legal community has a clique, "contracts are made to be broken."

But to the Easter man, a covenant was never to be broken, and a blood covenant broken meant the death of the one who broke it. Remember when Joshua and the Israelites were defeating armies bigger and better equipped than they were because God was honoring his covenant with them and one person broke the covenant and was killed with his wife and children by Joshua in Joshua chapter 7. Blood covenants were called that because of the blood that was shed to institute them and for the price exacted for breaking it.

Let's look at what the disciples "heard" with their Eastern ears and understanding when Jesus cut the blood covenant with them on this night.

As Jesus broke the bread and gave it to them in covenant, he said the following, "This bread represents me, all that I am and have materially. I commit to you all that I have in heaven and on earth. It is now as much yours as it is mine. Ask anything of me from this point on, and I will give it to you. There is nothing I will ever withhold from you if you ask. In fact, since I am going back to heaven and will be administering this covenant from my throne there, I will not only give you whatever you ask for, I'll also commit to you right now that if I don't have it, I'll create it for you.

"Now if you want to enter into this covenant I'm offering, then all that you have materially is mine for the asking as well, and I can call on you to give it to me at any time or to anyone I designate. If you break this bread with me, you will have entered into this covenant with me. Do you understand that all that is mine is yours and all that is yours is mine? If so, break and eat!"

They all agreed to do this, even Judas.

Now the cup: Jesus said the wine represented his blood. And what did the disciples hear?

"By partaking of the wine and calling it my blood of the new covenant, I am sealing forever the promises I have made to you with my very blood. I will lay down my life for you. I freely give my life for you and for all men who will enter into covenant with me as you are. As this was a free will act of mine, so it must be for you. If you drink of this cup with me, you are saying in covenant that your life is mine to do with as I see fit. You will be agreeing to lay down your life for me, just as I have agreed to lay down my life for you. If you are willing to do that, then drink. If not don't drink! Don't agree to do something that you won't do. Because this is a covenant unto death and to agree to keep it and then to not keep your promise means death."

Perhaps now we have a better understanding of communion:

Wherefore whosoever shall eat this bread, and drink this cup of the Lord, unworthily, shall be guilty of the body and blood of the Lord.

But let a man examine himself, and so let him eat of that bread, and drink of that cup.

For he that eateth and drinketh unworthily, eateth and drinketh damnation to himself, not discerning the Lord's body.

For this cause many are weak and sickly among you, and many sleep. (1 Cor. 11:27–30)

I would that no one would take the Lord's Supper until they have been properly instructed in honor of the Lord, his covenant and for their own benefit. Wouldn't you agree now?

Questions:

1. Have I accepted the traditions of man and made them more important than the word of God, thus voided the power of God's word in my life?
2. Am I now willing to trust and accept God's plan for my life over my own?
3. Am I now willing to enter into covenant with the Lord Jesus in a "blood covenant" relationship?

Activity:

Read John chapters 12–17 in preparation for chapter 5.

ENTERING THE GARDEN

Then cometh Jesus with them unto a place called Gethsemane, and saith unto the disciples, Sit ye here, while I go and pray yonder. (Matt. 26:36)

A single step for Jesus. All He has to do is open the gate, take one little step over the portal into the garden. But, oh, what a step! This step, if carried to its completion, will change the entire world for all time.

It is the step from the ministry of Jesus to the ministry to Jesus. He pauses. This step is what He came into the world to take, but it is no longer a step into a garden of peace. Rather, it is a step into His own personal garden of total submission of His humanness. The flesh must die, for the spirit to live.

This is the moment of truth!

He feels the fear of the unknown!

He feels the fear of the known!

His trust in the Father is tested!

The possibility of forfeiting occurs in his mind!

I believe all of us are offered this step of submission, this "death decision" that Jesus referred to when He said:

> *For many are called, but few are chosen. (Matt. 22:14)*

We all come to a point in our Christian walk when we have to decide if we will accept our garden, not for comfort, but for crucifying the flesh. This is the death we Christians must experience. It's the only death for us because

> *We know that we have passed from death unto life, because we love the brethren. He that loveth not his brother abideth in death. (1 John 3:14)*

Our secure and serene place of prayer and communion with our loving Heavenly Father is the very place where the Spirit of God calls us to make this decision. We have always enjoyed the fellowship, walking and talking with our Lord. Oh, He felt so close we could almost touch Him. But then He asks for our commitment, our death to self, and we turn aside. Remember the rich young ruler? Jesus didn't mince words. He cut to the core problem. He said the following:

> *Then Jesus beholding him loved him, and said unto him, One thing thou lackest: go thy way, sell whatsoever thou hast, and give to the poor, and thou shalt have treasure in heaven: and come, take up the cross, and follow me. (Mark 10:21)*

He demands we give up whatever stands between us and our total commitment to Him.

Are you willing to take the next step in your walk with the Lord? This is not the place for weak-kneed weekend warrior Christians. Just like a plant we either grow or die. Oh, I don't mean you'll lose you salvation:

> *My sheep hear my voice, and I know them, and they follow me:*
>
> *And I give unto them eternal life; and they shall never perish, neither shall any man pluck them out of my hand.*
>
> *My Father, which gave them me, is greater than all; and no man is able to pluck them out of my Father's hand. (John 10:27–29)*

However, God is not going to take us any deeper into His treasure house of blessings unless, or until, we willingly take that one step over the portal into our garden of submission, commitment, and death.

Maybe you are the businessman who dipped his toe into the Jordan River and felt a move of God on his life, but did not believe it would be good for business if he took some of his profits and supported a missionary. After all "I might need extra funds if sales began to slow down." Then he wonders why they do.

Or maybe you are the housewife who could not find the time to meet with a group of ladies from church to pray one afternoon a week for revival in her town, but found time to demonstrate in front of an adult book store and got arrested for her trouble.

Maybe you are the salesman who could not get up at 5:00 a.m. one day a month to pray with a group of men for God's direction and blessings, but makes sure to be up by 4:00 a.m. any time a friend calls to join a few buddies for a fishing expedition.

Are you the clerk who hides her Christianity so she won't be asked questions that might embarrass her?

It happens thousands, no, millions of times a day all over the world. Opportunities to say a word, to perform an act of kindness, showing forth Gods love to a hateful world, to make a difference, because it calls for a decision, a commitment, a dying to self for the glory of God. Once this step is taken, there is no turning back because we have stopped trusting in ourselves and our way of doing and thinking, and must live in raw trust in our Father! No more me, all you, Father.

As Jesus contemplates stepping over that portal, His mind recalled every previous visit, the times alone with His Father. "I sat on that rock while He showed Me I'd heal the woman in the temple bowed down under the penalty of sin for eighteen years."

> *And, behold, there was a woman which had a spirit of infirmity eighteen years, and was bowed together, and could in no wise lift up herself.*
>
> *And when Jesus saw her, he called her to him, and said unto her, Woman, thou art loosed from thine infirmity.*
>
> *And he laid his hands on her: and immediately she was made straight, and glorified God. (Luke 13:11–13*

"And that tree is the one I rested against while the Father told Me what to do in raising Lazarus from the dead."

And when he thus had spoken, he cried with a loud voice, Lazarus, come forth. (John 11:43)

Then answered Jesus and said unto them, Verily, verily, I say unto you, The Son can do nothing of himself, but what he seeth the Father do: for what things so ever he doeth, these also doeth the Son likewise. (John 5:19)

This is where Jesus had spent His times of enjoyment and His times of refreshment, and now this same place is to become His place of decision, commitment, submission, and death of the human, the flesh. The Adamic nature must die. The disciple is not greater than the master; therefore, it is the same for you and me. God always uses our place of prayer and communion as our place of decision and submission, just as it was for our Lord.

Jesus, the Son of God, had known this was the cup He would drink from the foundation of the earth, and now Jesus the Son of Man in His humanness will be tested again. The testing in the wilderness was the first test of the second Adam. This will be the last and most severe test. This is the one that will affect all mankind for all time. Remember the real test of Adam? When his wife offered the forbidden fruit, he, Adam, had to make a decision: to accept the fruit meant turning his back on his Father, God, and it meant all offspring would be alienated from God the Father. But to refuse the fruit meant to deny his wife, his flesh:

Therefore shall a man leave his father and his mother, and shall cleave unto his wife: and they shall be one flesh. (Gen. 2:24)

And, as we already discussed, he chose the flesh.

He has not reached His rock of prayer yet, nor have His prayers been spoken. He is just now ready to step into the garden. He remembers the board meeting between Him the Father and the Holy Spirit, when this part of the plan of redemption was decided upon. It seemed perfect then and does now, but the flesh is beginning to recoil from this step. Perhaps before He takes this step He takes an inventory of recent events. Everything that needed to be said has been said. All that the Father had asked Him to do up to this point in their plan had been completed. All duties are finished. The final instructions have been given to the disciples, including some rather poignant admonitions. The time has come for the completion of all righteousness, just as he said to John before being baptized:

And Jesus answering said unto him, Suffer it to be so now: for thus it becometh us to fulfill all righteousness. Then he suffered him. (Matt. 3:15)

Have you ever made a decision, opened a door or a gate that in opening you knew you were closing another door, or perhaps all other doors? Jesus is about to do just that. There was security in the garden and in His life before this garden experience.

It is always easier to talk about what you are going to do, than to do it. It is always easier to talk about what you are going to suffer when it is in the future than to face it when it is time to suffer. Now the horror of it all hits Jesus, the Son of Man, and it makes His knees buckle. It paralyzes His reason, it tests His sanity, and it brings out the frailty of His humanity. His human reasoning engages and tries to reason with the inner man. He remembers the words of Mordecai to Queen Esther:

For if thou altogether holdest thy peace at this time, then shall there enlargement and deliverance arise

> *to the Jews from another place; but thou and thy*
> *father's house shall be destroyed: and who knoweth*
> *whether thou art come to the kingdom for such a*
> *time as this? (Ester 4:14)*

He finds no comfort in that thought because He *knows* He must go forward. This is the moment for which He was brought into the world.

> *I came forth from the Father, and am come into*
> *the world: again, I leave the world, and go to the*
> *Father. (John 16:28)*

There is no question about His purpose for being on this earth. He had been telling His disciples for a long time that He would suffer and die for the redemption of mankind. But now He has to face it.

As God, it was the reason for the incarnation.

As man, it was too horrible to consider.

As God, it was the only way to bring man back into right standing with God.

As man, was it worth the price?

Psychiatrists tell us the closest a sane person comes to insanity is the split second before a decision is made on an important matter. We see that moment coming to the human Jesus right now. He has the option, the right. The Father gave him that right. It is called free will. We have it too. We can refuse to do God's will, and all too often, do. Jesus can refuse to go forward, but if he stops now.

Then He acts!

He knows the decision He is making as He plants his foot firmly in the garden of Gethsemane.

Questions:

1. What times can you recall when you knew God was talking and you did not heed?
2. Have you had a change of heart? A heart of flesh for one of stone?
3. Has the time come for you to let the flesh die, so Christ can live through you?

Activity:

Write out a simple commitment prayer of what you are willing *now* to do, something that you will do, and then ask the Father to help you. Then do it.

O Father God I have chased after money all my live, and here I am at seventy-six years of age and need to keep working just to pay the bills. I give up! Today I commit myself to seek first your kingdom and trust you to add all the things I need for life and godliness. Amen.

CHAPTER 6

A WALK IN THE GARDEN

When Jesus had spoken these words, he went forth with his disciples over the brook Cedron, where was a garden, into the which he entered, and his disciples. (John 18:1)

Do you have a best friend? I do. In January 1964, I met Dave when I went to work for Encyclopedia Britannica in Omaha, Nebraska. We traveled together, went through divorces together, we dated together. In fact I remember one time he lined me up with a motor-cycle-wearing tough gal, who was the friend of a girl he wanted to date, and I endured the evening because Dave was my best friend. We have played together, worked together, laughed together, and cried together for over fifty years.

When I married Nita, he met and married her best friend Barbara. I was the one he called when he found out his mother Lois was dying of cancer and had only ninety days to live. Dave wanted to talk to me when his son Danny and his wife were killed July 17, 1996, in the TWA 800 crash.

God gave me a poem for him. I prayed with him, and I wept with him. God used me to talk with him and to pray with and for him as he walked through his "valley of the shadow of death." Of all my friends and acquaintances, only Dave wrote to me almost every week while I was in prison. God used him to brighten my life and encouraged me when I needed it. Only Nita and my mother wrote more often. Dave is my best friend.

My *very* best friend is Nita, my wife. There are things I will not share with anyone but Dave and Nita, just as Nita has things she will only share with Barbara and me. They are best friends just as Dave and I are. But there are things, feelings, and fears that I will only share with Nita, my very best friend because God made us one flesh. And when I talk to her, it's like talking to the rest of me. I believe when you truly understand God's plan for a husband and wife and accept His plan, your spouse will become your very best friend, forever. We don't love our friends, Dave and Barb, any less. We just have a different kind of relationship and love for each other.

What is a friend? There are as many definitions as there are friends, I suppose, but to me a friend is someone whom you can share common interests with, someone you can trust and love. A friend is someone you can share your hurts with, as well as your joys, and someone who loves you in spite of your faults. The prodigal son had lots of "friends" while his money lasted, but when his money was gone, so were his friends.

Jesus also had lots of friends during His miraculous ministry, thousands of them. He had seventy close friends, disciples, whom He sent out as special messengers to announce the coming of His kingdom

After these things the Lord appointed other seventy also, and sent them two and two before his face

into every city and place, whither he himself would
come. (Luke 10:1)

There was the "inner circle," the twelve, then the special three, Peter, James, and John. Yet in the end He will be alone with His Father, and so are we at times of great trial. Even our very best friends cannot save us, redeem us, or deliver us. They can only help bring us to the place of decision. The ultimate decisions of life are always between the Father and the child, alone.

When our grandson Nicholas Dumke was going into the Marines, I gave him a Bible and in the front, I wrote, "Nick, there will be a time in your life when your comrades will not be enough, your friends will not be enough, nor will your family. Only God will be enough. I want you to seek him in everything you do, and he will protect you and your comrades."

(Note: Nick came home, safe and sound, and so did his buddies.)

Now there are only eleven disciples, for one of his friends had betrayed him.

But, behold, the hand of him that betrayeth me is
with me on the table. (Luke 22:21)

As He enters the garden, the horror of this night in Gethsemane begins to grip Him. The pain, the grief, the terror is too much to share with any but the closest of friends. He needs a friend who He can lean on, perhaps lay His head upon as John had done to Him as they ate at the Passover. So He tells the eight to stay by the gate. But he did not ask them to pray.

Then cometh Jesus with them unto a place called
Gethsemane, and saith unto the disciples, Sit ye
here, while I go and pray yonder. (Matt. 26:36)

I recall a story about a pastor who was in the hospital quite sick and he asked his wife to have the prayer meeting group pray for him one night. Well, they did, and he told someone later that he had been mending quite well until that night during the prayer meeting. While the good folk from the church were praying for him, he almost died and he could not understand it until one of the people who had been doing the praying said, "Well, Pastor, we didn't know how to pray, so we just prayed that if you were to die that your passing would be easy and that your widow would be able to endure without you."

The pastor said, "That bunch liked to have killed me with their prayers!"

Be careful who you ask to pray for you. You may not like what they pray, and Jesus knew that and knows the hearts of all men. He knows yours too, you know! So He left the eight to sit, but not to pray. And now the walk through the garden begins with His three best friends.

And he taketh with him Peter and James and John, and began to be sore amazed, and to be very heavy; (Mark 14:33)

The Greek word the translators rendered "sore amazed" is *ekthambeo*, which means "to throw into terror, alarm, and distress."

Why would the son of God, our Lord and God, be in terror of anything? Why? Because the Son of Man, Jesus, is walking this walk and drinking this cup as a man, not as God. The very human Jesus must face his trial, His test, and His death as a man, just the same as you and I have to face our trials, our sufferings, our pain, and, ultimately, our own death. He was tested in all ways as we are:

For we have not an high priest which cannot be touched with the feeling of our infirmities; but was

*in all points tempted like as we are, yet without
sin. (Heb. 4:15)*

We are human, so was He. What we see occur in the next few
hours should give us strength and remove the guilt and condemna-
tion of failure we have struggled with when we stumbled in the past
and when we do now.

Please allow me to take a little literary license or liberty here
because we don't speak in Elizabethan English today as they did when
this was translated in the sixteenth century, and I believe there are
times when a sentence was used to express an idea or whole thought.
Allow me to tell you what I hear. The very human Jesus is saying
something like what was in letter I received from my love when we
found out that my parole hearing would not be in one month, but
in nine months.

"The heartache, the loneliness, utter desolation, worry, fear,
sadness. Oh, the sadness! Like a heavy cloth has been dropped over
me, weighing me down, making me so very, very weary, hard to
move, to lift my arm, my head. If only I could crawl deep into the
closet and hide, hide, hide for a very long time. But we won't hide.
We will go on!"

Jesus was human and suffered with "like passions" just like we
do, and sometimes we suffer just like He did. Have you ever thought
of that? Sometimes we suffer or have the same feelings Jesus had. As
Jesus walked through the garden, he had to have his closest friends
help him because the Son of Man was too weak to walk without
leaning on a friend.

He is almost to that special place where He has met the Father
so many times before, the Rock, but the pain is too intense, the bur-
den too great, to allow even his closest and best friends to accompany
Him, not even the three. He stops and says, almost in a whisper,

Then saith he unto them, My soul is exceeding sorrowful, even unto death: tarry ye here, and watch with me.

And he went a little further, and fell on his face, and prayed, saying, O my Father, if it be possible, let this cup pass from me: nevertheless not as I will, but as thou wilt. (Matt. 26:38–39)

I have read commentaries that suggest that this great struggle was Satan's last attempt to kill Jesus before He could get to the cross and redeem man. I guess that is a possibility, but it does not seem plausible to me, because on each earlier attempt on His life, Jesus's composure and response was different. He would walk away from those who wished Him harm, like you or I would walk away from a conversation.

No, I believe this is very different. This is the great struggle Jesus, the Son of Man, had to win as a man in order for Jesus, the Son of God and the Son of Man, to become the sacrifice to redeem all of mankind. If He failed here, as the first Adam had, God's man was lost forever without a redeemer. If Jesus couldn't win over sin and Satan, no one could.

God gave Jesus the right, the covenant right, to ask for and receive deliverance. This will help us when we have found scriptures to stand on for promises of God and have prayed and believed, and it seemed nothing happened. Consider: Jesus could have claimed deliverance by the Abrahamic covenant, the Mosaic covenant, the Davidic covenant, or the Psalms, Proverbs, or any of the prophets. He could have called an angelic host to rescue Him, but He chose to obey his call.

There is a step that must be taken after our claim, but before we receive the answer, and that is what Jesus is about to do at the rock of decision.

Let's not get into foolishness here. It is always God's will to save us, to heal us, and to deliver us. These rights were bought and paid for legally at Calvary. Period. But we are free moral agents as Jesus was, and as such the Father will allow us to make our own decisions. We will reap the harvest of those decisions, good or bad, but He will never force us to do anything. And He was not going to force Jesus, Son of Man, to do what Jesus, Son of God, knew He was sent to do. Jesus did not have to go to the cross. He did not have to die.

> *No man taketh it from me, but I lay it down of myself. I have power to lay it down, and I have power to take it again. This commandment have I received of my Father. (John 10:18)*

He died willingly for us, but to do it He had to fight and win this battle, and in doing so He gives us an example to follow when we are facing hard decisions.

Questions:

1. Have I reached an understanding of the one flesh relationship God ordained between my husband/wife and myself?
2. Is my wife/husband my very best friend?
3. Have I developed a deep personal relationship with the Father so I know where to go in time of great distress?
4. Am I willing to let God have His way with me?

Activity:

Take time to develop a close father and son relationship with the Father.

Take time to develop that "we are one" covenant love with your spouse.

CHAPTER 7

THE ROCK OF PRAYER AND DECISION

If I could just reach the rock!

Can't move.

The human Jesus is frozen with fear.

"Father!" he cries out.

> *And he went a little further, and fell on his face, and prayed, saying, O my Father, if it be possible, let this cup pass from me: nevertheless not as I will, but as thou wilt.(Matt. 26:39)*

> *Saying, Father, if thou be willing, remove this cup from me: nevertheless not my will, but thine, be done.*

> *And there appeared an angel unto him from heaven, strengthening him. (Luke 22:42–43)*

Obedience regardless of consequences.

The angels speak:

"The Father sends his love."

"Yes, I know the Father loves me."

"The Father restores your soul.

Great and wonderful is our God.

The eye of the Lord is upon you, for you reverence Him.

You sought the Lord. He heard you and is delivering you from all your fears.

Not from the trial but from the fear."

As the messengers from his Father's throne continued to feed Jesus with the words of life, God's words, His strength was renewed but the pleading continued. Jesus had seen countless men crucified and knew this fate awaited Him. The spirit he received from his Father was willing to go through with their plan: the plan that He, Jesus, would once and for all time cancel the sin problem. The natural man, the Adamic nature He received from his mother Mary, was in rebellion.

What happens over the next three hours is significant and reveals the process that must take place in all human lives in order for the life of God to take over the life of flesh and for us to be one with the Father in all ways.

I see Jesus the man not able to do what he knows must be done without help from above. The same is true with us. I see Jesus pleading for one hour. Pleading that what he knows must be done be avoided. If we could have heard his first commitment to the Father's will, I believe it would have sounded like ours does sometimes, half-hearted. Notice how he talks to the disciples after that first hour.

And he cometh, and findeth them sleeping, and saith unto Peter, Simon, sleepest thou? couldest not thou watch one hour?

Watch ye and pray, lest ye enter into temptation.
The spirit truly is ready, but the flesh is weak.

And again he went away, and prayed, and spake
the same words. (Mark 14:37–39)

Now He kneels again. "Oh, Father, how we have planned for this hour to come, yet I must confess my flesh is weak. The human me does not want to go through this. If it be possible for us to remove the sin problem without my paying the price, please do it! Nevertheless, not my will, but thine be done."

Then He stands and goes to where He left His disciples.

And when he returned, he found them asleep
again, (for their eyes were heavy,) neither wist they
what to answer him. (Mark 14:40)

"Oh, Father"
The pleading continues, but the tone has changed.

Saying, Father, if thou be willing, remove this cup
from me: nevertheless not my will, but thine, be
done.

And there appeared an angel unto him from
heaven, strengthening him.

And being in an agony he prayed more earnestly:
and his sweat was as it were great drops of blood
falling down to the ground. (Luke 22:42–44)

And he cometh the third time, and saith unto them,
Sleep on now, and take your rest: it is enough, the
hour is come; behold, the Son of man is betrayed
into the hands of sinners. (Mark 14:41)

Jesus had to have the same faith in God that we must have. It is so easy to have faith when everything is going according to plan—that is, *your* plan. But when everything you trusted in holding together falls apart, what will you do?

This is the time for raw trust or faith in the shadows of life. It was during this time of shadow living that the Lord gave me the following words of encouragement in my prayer time and the poems "Faith in the Shadows" and "Walking with God in the Rain."

Faith in the Shadows

It's The Faith In The Shadows That Pleases Me
Not The Faith That Shouts "Oh Glory Be"
Or The One That Glories In Faith Received,
No, It's The Faith In The Shadows That Pleases
Me.

It's The Faith In The Shadows That Pleases Me,
It's The Faith Lived In Sorrow When You Still
Believe, It's Faith When You Don't Feel Or See,
It's The Faith Of, Faith In Me That Pleases Me.

It's The Faith In The Shadows That Pleases Me,
The Faith In The Valley, The Pit And Dread,
When The Night's Evil Powers And Fears Seem
Real, When The "What If's" Of Doubt Have All
Been said,

When Fear Of Loss Seems A Reality,
But Your Faith Stays Strong And Real In Me.
That 's The Faith Of The Shadows, And It Pleases
Me.

When It Seems Your Life Has Been A Waste, And
It Seems That You Can Never Keep Pace, When
Faith Seems Weak And All Is Lost, Stop And
Consider Jesus' Cost
Too Give You The Faith Of Victory.

It's Your Faith In The Shadows That Sets You Free,
(John Dumke, 11/13/95)

Walking with God in the Rain

The Eye Of The Lord Travels O'er The Earth
To Find A Man He Can Trust,
Seldom A Man Of Wealth Or Fame Or A Man
Who Thinks Too Much.
No, He Seeks A Man Of Broken Heart Who Feels
The Fathers Pain,
A Man Who Hides His Hurt and Tears By Walking
With God In The Rain.
(John Dumke, 11/11/95)

Questions:

1. Have you had a "close encounter" with God?
2. Is your life still all about you? Or have you let Him take over?

Activity:

Open the door of self (Jesus is knocking) and let Him in. The choice is yours. The benefit is eternity with God the Father, God the Son, and God the Holy Spirit! Wow!

CHAPTER 8

RUSH TO JUDGMENT

First, I want to say that although I'm going to use comparisons between my personal experiences and those of Jesus, I'm not placing myself on an equal plane with Him either in the severity of the charges, the penalty, nor the fierceness of the adversary. But rather as we look at the human emotions and His responses to them as opposed to mine, it may help us understand and learn what real trust in a loving Heavenly Father means.

With submission comes resolve.

Because all things were made by Him, He knew every attribute of the human and He knew the strength that would be required and would be given His human side with the power of God-given resolve and determination acquired in prayer. He also knew the end from the beginning: therefore

> *Looking unto Jesus the author and finisher of our faith; who for the joy that was set before him endured the cross, despising the shame, and is set down at the right hand of the throne of God. (Heb. 12:2)*

Once the Adamic nature was set aside, allowed—no, made—to die, His eye of faith could see or visualize the glory. It wasn't anywhere to be seen by the natural eye; but it was real, more real, than anything on planet Earth. It had to become real for the mind and body to live through the ordeal that was about to begin. If you've never been to prison, it's going to be hard for you to understand what I'm about to tell you, but try. Try to picture yourself in this story. Don't think of me, think of you.

It starts suddenly but works on you gradually until it takes over your every waking and sleeping thought. I can think of no more frightening words than "I have a warrant for your arrest." Everything safe in your life stops, disappears, and drops from sight. It's like you are dangling over a pit and you don't know how long you can hold on. Then your hand slips, and you know life is over. You are falling into nothingness, or something of which you have no concept, and you are more frightened than you've ever been before.

What does it all mean? Maybe it's a mistake, just a nightmare. Please I want to wake up!

When I heard those words, "Are you John Dumke?"

"Yes."

"Mr. Dumke, we have a warrant for your arrest."

My mind froze. My knees buckled. My voice sounded squeaky and my mouth was dry.

Because I started a business that the legal community didn't like (I sold living trusts that helped people avoid the legal cost of probate, therefore costing the attorneys a large part of their income). Through two cease and desist orders, they forced me to close my business. We lost our home, cars, credit, good name; and if that wasn't enough, now they were taking away my freedom.

Is this still America?

If I could have called for seventy-two thousand angels, as Jesus could have, they would have been called with my first words.

There are no words to describe the terror, the horror. I saw my wife's knees give way as she grabbed the countertop to steady herself. Even now it's hard for me to talk about that event: the pain is too great and too deep. The rest is a blur of arrest, bonds, a frightening three years of postponements, then, finally, a trial, appeal, and prison. We treat our animals with more respect and care than our prisoners. I know. I've been there.

But Jesus!

Where I recoiled, Jesus stepped forward. Where I was gripped with fear, He walked in faith. Where I would have been willing for someone else to take my place, He asked that His friends be allowed to go their way and He, Jesus, the one who could have killed them all with His word, took all their blame and ultimately paid the price of sin for them—and for you and me.

The obedient sacrifice.

"But, Lord, you don't understand! What they are doing to me is so unfair and illegal too!"

"Me too, John."

"But, Lord, they are just a bunch of unjust, unrighteous, bureaucratic lawyers twisting and perverting the law to fit their desires because I had a business that they didn't like. My business was costing them their big fees, so they are out to get even with me. Lord, can't you see that?"

"Me too, John."

"At the trial, Lord, I knew I was doomed. I saw it on the faces of everyone!"

"Me too, John."

"Lord, the sheriff who transported me to the county jail from which I was sent to prison told me, 'John, there was no way you were leaving our county without a guilty verdict and a maximum sentence. That was decided before you ever went to trial!'"

"Me too, John."

"Lord, I'm entering prison. I'm standing here naked, exposed, despised, reviled, taunted."

"Me too, John. I know the feeling. But at least you weren't beaten."

"Yes, Lord. I'm sorry, Lord. I submit to you, Lord, and your plan for my life. But, Lord, it hurts so badly. "

"I know. John. I know."

Jesus's trial?

A mockery at best, illegal, with a decision was made before conviction.

"I know, Lord, I know."

Question from Jesus:

"What hurt the most, John?"

Answer:

"The unbelief of my innocence by some people close to me. My wife, Nita Raye, our children, my parents, Nita's mom, and a few friends always believed in me. But others? There was no reason to try to argue the facts. People had made up their minds, and nothing I could say would change that."

"Live with it, John. I had to."

Now I understand why Jesus said so little. Everyone had already heard His words. If they didn't believe Him before, they won't believe Him now.

Be still and know that I am God

The spirit of God gave me over a hundred poems during my solitude. The following are a sample. Each one comes with a lesson for living for Him.

CHAPTER 9

A SKULL

The Mount Of Olivet
A Name So Grand,
It's Place In History,
Part Of God's Plan.

Our savior sat Down
On Its Crown To Preach,
When Crowds Pressed In
He Paused, To Heal And Teach.

And Then The Garden,
It Was Here He Groaned,
Sometimes With Friends,
Sometimes Alone.

Another Hill
Not Far Away,
The Place Of The Skull,
Would Have It's Day.

"Why Me Lord,
Why Chose Me For Shame?"
"Mouths Spit Out "Golgotha,"
And Despise My Name."

"I Should Have Been Pretty
Grassed, Treed And Tall,
Instead Folks Remember
Because Of Mans Fall."

"I Chose You For Beauty,
Only I Could See,
Then Changed Your Name,
To "Calvary."

"All Through The Ages
People Will To You, Bow,
Not For Your Beauty,
But The Blood On Your Brow."

So 'Tis With Us,
Not Beauty Nor Fame,
But Whether We'll Carry
Our Cross, In His Name.

Will We Stop Striving
For Things That Will Die,
And Submit To Our savior,
Eternity To Buy?

Or Does Adam's Sin
Still Lurk In Our Bones?

Have We Not Learned,
Still Call, This Place, Home?

Come, Learn Children,
A Lesson From Me,
I, Wisdom Know
What's Best, You'll See

It's Simple, Really
Its Not Very Hard,
God Loves His Man,
Tho He's, Sin Marred.

Think For A Minute,
Of All That He's Done,
He's Prepared Our New Home,
And He's Sent Us His Son,

To Tell The Sweet Story
Of A Father's Love Lost,
Of A Redemption Plan,
And Of The Life It Cost.

Of A Plan So Great
Angels Looked In Awe,
That Love Would Replace
A Multitude Of Law.

"So You See, Little Hill
You're A Part Of My Plan,
You Had A Role To Play
In The Redemption Of Man."

'Tho Your Name Was, "A Skull."
Cruel Death, Your History,
Because Of Son Jesus
People Praise "Calvary."

So It Is With You,
So It Is With Me.
Sometimes God's Grace
Is In What We Can't See.

Remember, You're His Child
Despise All The Shame,
Believe In His Word,
Honor His Blessed Name.

You're Just A Part,
But Important Too,
He'll Change Your Name,
And Give Honor To You.

Trust In His Love,
Obey His Call,
Rest In His Love
He's Our, All In All!
(John Dumke, 12/13/95)

It doesn't make any difference what people say about you, when they berate you, or even curse you, because God has a plan for your life and He will bring it to fruition, if you will surrender and allow Him. Even Jesus, as He was growing up, was called a bastard child because His mother, Mary, was found to be with child before she and Joseph married.

Think about it, God used that "condition" to protect His son.

What you are going through now is simply God preparing you to fit into his place for you in His plan.

CHAPTER 10

JACOB AND
HIS LAMB

I wrote is short story about a lad and his lamb set at the time of the crucifixion of Jesus.

Jacob awoke to the soft touch of a lamb's tongue, and he smiled. "Good morning, Little Shadow," he murmured and placed his arm around his pet lamb.

What a week he had, had. As a Jewish boy, his bar mitzvah was the most exciting event of his life, up till now, and one he had looked forward to for as long as he could remember because now he was a man.

What a celebration his father had prepared for him. All his friends were there and his father's friend. And everyone was congratulating him and welcoming him into manhood, and oh what fun with singing and dancing and then the introduction.

His father Eli had quieted all the guests, and with his big booming voice, he said, "I want all our friends and family to greet my son Jacob who pleases me very much because he is a good son and an obedient son. Greet him no longer as a child because today he is a man."

Everyone cheered and patted him on the back and hugged and kissed him, and well, it was almost too much to bear. And even now, thinking about it, he was both embarrassed by all the attention and thrilled by the new status he had attained. Even sweet Rebecca had danced with him, and when no one was looking, she took his hand and held it.

Now he thought he understood what his father and friends meant when he had heard them pray, "I thank you, O God, that I was born a man." In fact, come to think of it, the next important happening in his life would be his wedding. He wondered, *Would it be to Rebecca?* Last week's excitement would have to carry him for quite a while.

He was a man, and that meant the educational duties of his mother were over. And from now on his father would take over teaching the new "man" he had become. As of now he would be included in the men's discussions and work and soon would begin intensive studies of the Torah. He already knew many of the Psalms. King David was his favorite ancestor. Yes, he had been looking forward to this day for as long as he could remember. No more snickers from the older boys because he was now one of them and no more sitting with his mother at the synagogue and being taught like one of the girls at his mother's knee. He was a man. Even Rebecca had seen that. Just the thought of it was enough to bring him to full wakefulness.

"Well, good morning again, Little Shadow, and an exciting morning it is, little one!"

Jacob guessed that no one knew what an attachment had grown between him and Shadow. Certainly not his father because he had strict instructions never to make a pet of any lamb. It increased their chances of disease, and if the lamb was needed for food or to sell, it makes the separating too hard to bear.

But no lamb had ever so touched his heart. He called him his lamb, and he could imagine one day Little Shadow being Big Shadow and the number one ram in his father's flock. Perhaps he would be the progenitor of his own flock as well. Shadow was six months old but still followed Jacob around like a shadow, just like he had almost since the day he was born. That was, of course, when he wasn't at his mother's side. In fact, that was how the lamb got his name, but then you probably already guessed that.

Jacob stood up and stretched and said, "Come on, Shadow, it's time for cakes and dates before we take the flock to the pasture."

And at that they marched off to see Mother for breakfast and a lunch to take with them to the hills.

It was the sixth hour, twelve o'clock noon, on this the fifth day of the week, the eighth of Abib. He and Little Shadow had led the flock to this area; and then, as they always did in the morning, they played together, just enjoying the thrill of being alive. Right now Jacob did not feel all grown-up. In fact he still felt like a child and thought, *I guess that's all part of growing up too.*

He was laughing and running with his friend until, finally exhausted, he and Little Shadow fell down, tumbling in the grass, and came to rest staring at the white billowing clouds floating across the sky. He thought how wonderful life was and how blessed he was by the Lord God. He thought of his ancestor, King David, *He was a shepherd boy, er, man like me once, and the Lord God blessed him with the kingdom of Israel! I wonder what the Lord God has in store for me.*

Jacob meditated on some of David's psalms for a while until he heard a noise that brought him back to reality. He jumped up, looked around, and then, just to be on the safe side, walked completely around the flock, looking in all directions until he was satisfied there was nothing threatening the sheep. Then he and Shadow sat down and had a drink, and Jacob shared a bite of his lunch with his friend, not much you understand, but enough so Shadow stayed close for a while before he went to have his own lunch.

That night Jacob's father told him that the next day, toward evening, he would come out to the pasture to select the sacrifice to take to the temple next week for Passover. He would have to do it on the ninth, a day early because the commanded day, the tenth, fell on the Sabbath. He, Eli, the father, would select the perfect lamb, then take the chosen one to the house to keep it safe and well fed until the fourteenth of Abib, the day the Lord God established through Moses as the day to kill the Passover, at the time of sacrifice, the ninth hour, 3:00 p.m. There Eli would present him to the priest as their families sacrifice, their Passover lamb.

If your family was too small to consume the entire animal in one meal, as was theirs, then you were to join your family with a neighbor or, as in their case, another family member, who was their next door neighbor, Eli's brother Stephen's family, so nothing would be wasted. Each year he had seen his father and Uncle Stephen leave for the temple with the lamb, and later that day, they would return with the carcass. Then his mother and aunt would prepare the Passover supper. One year they would eat at their home and the next at Uncle Stephen's, and this year it was Eli's turn, so Jacob was doubly excited.

This was Jacob's favorite feast with the closeness of family, good food, and the story of how the Lord God delivered their ancestors from bondage in Egypt; and how Jacob loved the story of the death angel "passing over" all the homes of his people because of the blood of the lamb protecting it. He especially liked it when his father would stand up and say, "One day the Lord God will send the Messiah, and He will provide an eternal sacrifice, and all our sins will be forgiven for all time, and we will never again have to offer blood sacrifices, for as was promised to our father Abraham, 'The Lord will provide Himself, a sacrifice.'"

Jacob was never quite sure what that meant but thought that as he began his new instructions in the Torah he would learn. Right now there was just so much to take in, all these new responsibilities and adventures that sleep was long in coming.

The next day Jacob was waiting for his father when he saw him coming. He had spent the day being a little more grown-up in manner just in case his father came early. In fact, he had hardly spent any time with Shadow, shooing him away if he spent too much time at Jacob's side. After all he was a man now, and he wanted to look manly for his father.

It had been an exhilarating day, and he was famished. The breeze was cool, but it felt good. And soon, he would be sitting in the warmth of their home, enjoying the evening meal, which was always his favorite part of the day.

Jacob's father began walking among the sheep with him and would occasionally stop and inspect a lamb to see if it was the one good enough, perfect for the Lord God while he explained the law.

"Jacob, hear me well, for one day you will need to explain all this to your son. The lamb we will take to the temple must be a male, at least eight days old but not over one year old, and must not have had any broken bones nor any spot or blemish. He must be the best we have, or he will not be worthy to be a sacrificial lamb to the Lord God."

Lamb after lamb was inspected by Eli and rejected until with pleased finality he said, "Here he is! This is the perfect lamb for God!"

He picked up a lamb and placed him on his shoulders and turned to head back to the house.

Jacob had just turned around to look over the flock before his father found the lamb, and as he turned back, he caught his breath and said, "But faith."

His words caught in his throat. He was suddenly dumb. He couldn't speak. His throat was dry, and no further sound came. For just a moment, he thought he would fall. His legs started to buckle. He wanted to argue, but he knew it would do no good, and he felt like his world had just crumbled. He felt the fire behind his eyes, and he couldn't stop the tears.

Eli turned to his son and said, "Jacob, I have told you many times not to make pets of the lambs. I hope you didn't disobey me and this one was too close to you."

When Eli saw the tears, he stopped admonishing his son and felt pity, remembering his own childhood and a lamb he loved and his father's words. With unusual tenderness but firmness, he talked to his son. "Jacob." He paused. "Son, I too loved a lamb when I was a lad like you, and I'm going to tell you what my father told me. The Lord God demands the best we have, not because He needs it or wants to hurt us but to help us understand the awfulness of sin and that the price or cost of redeeming us from the penalty of it has to be high.

"Starting in the garden of Eden, He ordained a sacrifice of innocence, a blood sacrifice to be a covering of our sins to enable us to have communion with Him. Son, I believe the Lord God allows us to feel some of the pain He feels when we are separated from Him by our disobedience, by the pain we feel at our loss. You, Jacob, are now a man and part of the responsibility you must begin to accept is the cost of the sacrifices, both the monetary and the emotional cost."

Eli watched his son and saw the maturing take place and saw again the price of sin. It hurt more than he would ever admit, but as a father, he knew he could not recant. The Lord God deserved the best, and for the blessings to be on his family, he could not knowingly give anything less, not even the second best. "You can sleep with him every night until Passover, if you want. But, son, he is our best."

Eli stood up, hugged his son, placed Little Shadow on his shoulders again, and headed back to the house.

Jacob watched his father and Shadow until they were out of sight. Then with a heavy heart he stood up and turned his face to his responsibility and an altogether too painful manhood. His arms seemed too long and so heavy. His legs felt like they weighed too much to move, and his head was so heavy so heavy he could hardly hold it up.

The breeze was cold and made him shiver. He had lost his hunger, and he stared fixedly at the flock, seeing them all yet acknowledging none of them. Right now he wasn't sure if he wanted to grow up. *How could a day that started with such joy have turned so sorrowful?*

Jacob didn't have the benefit of having someone explain grief, depression, loss, loneliness, or the fact that this too will pass. All he knew, right now today, was he missed his friend, and soon, too soon, his friend would be gone forever.

Jacob was sure the Sabbath meal was as good as it always was, but he could not eat. The stars were just as bright, but he did not see them. There was still love in his heart, but he could not express it. The pain was so great it had numbed him, and that he could not understand.

He slept with Little Shadow that night, and the next, and the next. The days were a blur of doing the duties and chores required of him and trying to pretend the world was the same, putting a smile on his face when his father was near and then letting the weight of the sorrow have its way with him.

Never will I love another lamb, he thought. *Never! It hurts too much!*

Welcome to life, Jacob! There is no pain as great as the pain of love, and love lost. There is no joy as great as the joy love can bring either, but there seems to be a trade-off. To experience the glory of love, we must be willing to expose ourselves to the possibility of the greatest kind of hurt.

Tuesday morning, Abib the thirteenth, tomorrow was the day of the sacrifice, and now Jacob wished he had spent more time with

Shadow. Time was so short. *Why didn't I use every moment to be with my friend?* But he knew, as we all know, it's hard to be close to the one who is causing the pain even when it's not their fault.

Today was different. Although Shadow was kept at home and safe from harm, Jacob spent as much time as possible with him and held his friend all night, awaking many times just to make sure Shadow was still there. Far too soon, it was morning, the day of the sacrifice.

Jacob went to the pasture with the flock and tended them, but his father was sending a hired hand to take over at noon so he could prepare to accompany his father and uncle as they took the lamb to the temple. Jacob had come to the place in his heart and mind of, if not peace, at least acceptance of the sacrifice; and he had decided that he would be the man his father wanted him to be and that the Lord God demanded.

The morning sped by too quickly and seemed to be filled with a sort of pallor or stillness that made life seem sort of unreal. Jacob thought for a brief moment that perhaps the whole world felt his pain.

And then something happened that was so frightening that his mouth turned dry and cold chills ran up and down his entire body. The sun disappeared. It was as dark as midnight. He thought he heard screams.

The sheep began to mill in fright, and Jacob called out to calm them and began to lead them back home. He didn't know what else to do. He met the hired man on the way, and they walked back to the sheepfold together. After securing the sheep and leaving the helper behind, Jacob ran to the house hoping his father would be there and he could explain everything to him.

Eli sat at the table looking very puzzled himself but assured his family that it probably was nothing and they needed to just continue as if nothing was different. He did say they would wait awhile before going to the temple, so after lunch Jacob played with his friend.

As the time of the sacrifice grew near, Eli felt he could wait no longer. He stood up and said, "Well, Jacob, I believe we better get started. It surely will get light soon, and we still must prepare the Passover." Then he arose, looking much more confident than he felt.

Jacob placed a small cord around Little Shadow's neck and knelt down to kiss and hug his friend one last time and to let his friend wash his face with his tongue. Then he stood up and joined his father at the door where Eli had been waiting.

They began walking in the direction of Uncle Stephen's home. The path seemed hard and long and very lonely, though his father was by his side and Shadow stayed close enough to brush Jacob's leg with each step, perhaps out of fear because of the strange darkness or the change he had sensed in his friend. Every few steps he would lick Jacob's hand. The tears were gone now, only the heartache remained as they approached his uncle's gate.

The light from the torch Eli carried cast eerie shadows in front of them as Uncle Stephen's form came into view. The greeting between brothers was intermixed with thoughts of what could have caused the darkness. Uncle Stephen said maybe it had something to do with the executions that had taken place today. It seemed as if a man some called a prophet had been crucified outside of the city in fact some of his followers had claimed he was the Son of God!

All this conversation Jacob heard but paid little attention too as he was considering asking his father if he could go back home now. He didn't think he was yet man enough to go all the way into the temple for the sacrifice. Then his eyes fell to his uncle's side, and there stood another lamb!

Eli saw the lamb at the same time and said, "Stephen, this is my year to supply the lamb. We ate the Passover at your house last year."

His brother laughed and answered, as any younger brother would, "Eli, you are getting old. Last year my wife's parents were visiting, and we had to eat here because my home is bigger, but you supplied the lamb. In fact, you selected one that was a little bigger than the rest so there would be enough to go around. Remember?"

Jacob's heart stopped beating for just a moment, then rushed to catch up. He opened his mouth to say something as his hand dropped down to touch his friend, but before a sound could escape his lips, his father spoke.

Eli's eyes turned to his son just as Jacob's head turned up to him, and he saw the hope, the question, and the trust in a loving father. And he said in a matter of fact a tone as he could muster, though his voice cracked, "Well, son, it looks like you better take Little Shadow home."

"You knew his name!" Then without thinking and without shame, Jacob fell to his knees and hugged his friend, his lamb. He didn't even try to hide the tears of joy.

Eli didn't want his son to see his tears of relief, so he said as he turned his head, "Jacob, why don't you just stay at home with your lamb and thank the Lord God for supplying a substitute?"

"A substitute! A substitute! That's what the other lamb was, a substitute!"

Jacob did not need to hear his father's offer twice. He removed the cord from Shadows neck, and they started for home. It was at that moment when he heard his uncle say it was already almost the ninth hour and they needed to hurry that the earth suddenly shuddered, as if with a chill, followed by a deadly silence as they all stood still frozen with fear. Then just as suddenly as it had disappeared, the sun reappeared. With the sun came a sigh and a little nervous laughter. Then as if to deny the dread they had felt, Eli and Stephen headed toward town lost in the discussion of the day's events.

Jacob and Shadow ran, skipped, and laughed all the way home. He was sure it was the joy in his heart bursting forth on all of God's creation that had caused the sun to appear, the birds to sing, and the air to smell so fresh you would have thought it had rained. All of life was wonderful again.

The Lord God had provided a substitute sacrifice, and joy would fill him forever. Never would he cease to praise the Lord for His love and grace. His sins were forgiven, and his friend did not have to die.

"I never knew the Lord loved me this much." Jacob began to sing a psalm. "The heavens declare the glory of God."

To the chief Musician, A Psalm of David. The heavens declare the glory of God; and the firmament sheweth his handywork. (Ps. 19:1)

CHAPTER 11

HELL: OUR DESTINY WITHOUT JESUS

And when Jesus had cried with a loud voice, he said, Father, into thy hands I commend my spirit: and having said thus, he gave up the ghost. (Luke 23:46)

To the human eye, this was a scene too often observed by the Jews: a Roman cross; the victim's dead or dying; and the family members in grief, weeping in utter despair. But at the foot of Jesus's cross, we see Mary, His mother; and her sister, the wife of Cleophas; Mary Magdalene; John, the beloved disciple; and many women. But where were the other disciples, especially Peter and James?

As he looks down on the few, He asks, "Where are the seventy who I sent out to do miracles? Where are my brothers and sisters? They should be here, if for no other reason than to comfort our mother. Where are the ten lepers I healed, or, for that matter, all the hundreds of people I healed? Where is the mother whose son I raised from the dead? Where is the son? Where is Lazarus?

"I'll be back in three days and then I'll show them. I'll show them what fools they are!"

No, you and I may have thought something like that, but not Jesus. Love never tries to get even.

The decision was made: the battle had been won in the garden. Now He was simply carrying out the plan. Oh, what faith it took right here! Consider the absolute trust Jesus has in the Father. Jesus says, "Father, into your hands." All that the Son had with the Father since before time is on the line. All that He was or ever would be He was placing in the Father's hand. For the next three days and nights, he would be in hell, suffering the pains of hell like all sinful men and without a way out unless and until the Father orders it.

Here is the example for us. I am convinced that the Father requires us to let go of the grip we have on our lives and fall into God's mercy. This is true trust. I call it "raw" trust.

For whosoever will save his life shall lose it: and whosoever will lose his life for my sake shall find it. (Matt. 16:25)

Let us follow Jesus with this prayer of submission.

"Father, into your hands I commend my spirit, soul, and body. Your will for me is what I want, and I trust you completely to do what is for my good and your glory. Amen."

Let us now look into the real world, the spirit world, where we will spend our eternity. Here we see some extra observers. To the right of Jesus, we see two angels waiting for the penitent thief to die so they can carry out Jesus's instructions and carry him to Abraham's bosom.

To the left of Jesus, we see Lucifer himself with his lieutenants and special guests anticipating that much awaited point in time, the period in history, the time when he, Lucifer, wins. Because when the Son of God dies, clothed in the sins and sicknesses of the whole world, legally he belongs to Satan the same as any other sinful man.

Satan and his assemblage have been waiting since the sixth hour, twelve o'clock noon, the moment the Father had taken the Holy Spirit away from the Son and covered Him with the sins of all mankind, from the sin in the garden of Eden to the last sin of the final act of rebellion. Then the Father covered the earth with darkness to hide the shame of his Son carrying that sin, just as he had covered his first son, Adam, with the skins of the sacrificed. The blood covered the sin; the other covered the shame. It was at that point that Jesus's spirit experienced death. Have you ever thought of Jesus dying spiritually? He did. He had to, or he could not have died physically.

"Just be patient," Satan tells himself. "Soon he'll be all mine. He should have taken my offer in the wilderness, but I'm so glad he didn't. Now I'll have him to add to my kings of the Jews collection in hell."

He had invited the seven demons Jesus had ordered out of Mary Magdalene and the legion He had sent into the herd of swine and as many others as could break away from other assignments, demons whom this Jesus had ordered around as if He thought He was somebody. The father below sneered, waiting for his moment of triumphant. Never had he seen anything that delighted him more. Imagine all the sin, hate, filthiness, and vileness of all the worst despots ever to have lived being placed on one man and you have a beginning of what Satan saw in Jesus.

As Jesus spoke His last words as a dying man, Satan spoke his first words of the victory that he in his pride knew was his: "All right, get ready, it's time!"

And when Jesus had cried with a loud voice, he said, Father, into thy hands I commend my spirit:

*and having said thus, he gave up the ghost. (Luke
23:46)*

A great cheer arose from the demonic gallery, and Satan himself stepped forward to take possession of the sin-infested spirit of this one called the Son of Man, Jesus.

Now Jesus's greatest ordeal was to take place to satisfy the court decree of heaven. This is what He asked to be spared of when He prayed in the garden. This is what He accepted as He left the garden. Now the torture of soul and spirit would begin, the horror of which had made him shudder in terror.

The assemblage was descending. Sin had sapped all of Jesus's strength. He was powerless to fight. Sin does that to us right here. When we accept sin and commit our lives to it, we no longer have the strength to fight. We wallow in it long enough to become servants to it. I like what Kenneth Copeland said one time, "Don't blame the sinner, he's doing the best he can with the spirit he has." Jesus trusts the Father with His eternity in simple faith, the faith of a child.

The taunting and jeers of this group were far more devastating than those of the Roman guards or the hate-filled Jews, and it continued relentlessly. The closer they drew to the entrance to hell, the louder the voices became as those who had been left behind joined in the chorus. Now the screams, the wailing, and the gnashing of teeth by the inhabitants filled the air and added to the despair and hopelessness of hell.

"Why does man prefer this to God's glory?"

Only because the liar has told them it doesn't exist.

Jesus looked to the right just before He entered the realm of the unholy and saw all the saints in Abraham's bosom awaiting their release. Did He see a look of longing and despair? Was it the same look He had seen on His mother's face and the faces of His other followers on Golgotha's hill? Didn't they understand He had to do this? Had they not read the Scriptures? Had they not listened to him?

He wanted to say, "Hold on a little longer. Believe in God. He is still in charge." But he had no strength to do it now. They would have to have faith in the Father, just as He must.

As he passed through the opening to hell, Satan began speaking in a sort of sing-song nasal, "I said I'd win. Look Jesus at my collection of souls. Now here we have one of your own disciples, Judas. We saved a special place for him because he was so obedient to my voice. And I have reserved the deepest and hottest room for you. It's the one you made for and reserved for *me*. It is the most torturous of all cells in my abode, and we are going to chain you there. Where is your power now, Lord Jesus?"

The words dripped with the pure venom of unbridled hate.

"We are going to take our time getting there because I want you to hear the taunts and feel the hate of every soul I hold. Just think, everyone had a chance to avoid coming here, but they preferred me to God. I tricked them. I win! All's fair in hate and war."

Then he laughed. His laughter, unknown in our world lest the unsaved run terror stricken into the arms of our Savior, was so vile, so filled with all, that is evil that as it spilled over the tiers of hell, each of his demons joined in the chorus of this insidious, hellish, hilarity; and Jesus shuddered.

This is what accompanied the entourage on their descent through hell's halls, and Jesus endured it for you and for me.

"You are going to see that I am the victor, Jesus. I am the winner. You'll have to bow your knee to me, just like the other kings of the Jews I have here. In fact, did you notice I have more of the kings of Israel than Jehovah does, and you are going to see every one of them as we pass by?

The Bible tells us that thirty-three kings "did evil in the eyes of God," starting with King Saul, as recorded in the following:

*So Saul died for his transgression which he com-
mitted against the LORD, even against the word of
the LORD, which he kept not, and also for asking
counsel of one that had a familiar spirit, to enquire
of it; (1 Chron. 10:13)*

*And he wrought evil in the sight of the LORD; but
not like his father, and like his mother: for he put
away the image of Baal that his father had made.*

*Nevertheless he cleaved unto the sins of Jeroboam
the son of Nebat, which made Israel to sin; he
departed not there from. (2 Kings 3:2–3)*

How many are held here? I don't know. God knows, but too
many. And Jesus's heart broke again and again as he wept over them,
as He had wept over the city of His kings. "Why, man, oh why would
you not listen to my prophets? Was the pleasure of sin for a season
worth the torment of hell for eternity?"

At last they arrived at the reserved place for Jesus, and Satan,
sounding more like a real estate salesman, showing off a new apart-
ment than the personification of evil, began in foul delight, "Jesus."
It sounded like the way he has taught man to curse using that precious name. "Jesus, here it is, your new home in my kingdom, the
kingdom of the eternally damned, and I even had a special sign made
to place over your gate. Take a good look at it. Jesus looked.

And set up over his head his accusation written,
THIS IS JESUS THE KING OF THE JEWS. *(Matt. 27:37)*

They shoved him inside, chained him in the most painful position possible, bolted and locked the gate, and placed the strongest

of Satan's guards one on each side to ensure his containment and to block any attempt to escape.

As Satan left Jesus to the attacks of the other residents, all God's creation who were here, those who He had created to spend eternity with Him, but who had chosen evil over godliness, began their barrage of hate, fear, envy, spite, vile language, filthiness, and rebuke. They continued to repeat what the one crucified with him, without repentance, asked:

> *And one of the malefactors which were hanged railed on him, saying, If thou be Christ, save thyself and us. (Luke 23:39)*

If they shouted that once they shouted it a thousand times, half in hopeful seriousness and half in unbelieving ridicule.

He had endured the physical and mental torture of humans. Now he was enduring the greater torment of mental and spiritual torture of all that hell could produce. There is no rhyme or reason to hatred whether on earth or in hell, only here it's the completely unbridled passion of hate, unrestrained, all enveloping, and all-consuming.

Just as God is love without conditions or restraint, and those who truly love God become infected with His love and grow into it until the day, praise God, when we will be like he is, love itself, so is Satan's hate. And all that fall prey to him become infected with all he is until they are hate itself like father, like son.

We've all seen hate in man. Some have seen it cloaked in judicial robes or in the three-piece suits of prosecutors more interested in their win record than in the justice they are sworn to uphold. Maybe you have seen it in a boss, a child, a neighbor, a coworker, or a mate. The phony smiles and the sneers are all the same. They hurt and kill, and they are ugly. Hate is sin, and it is ugly. But wait, perhaps you have also seen it in the mirror! I did, and I didn't like it. And I didn't want it anymore, so I asked our Father to replace it with love, and he did! He will, you know, if you ask him in faith.

Resolve to Wait on God

Be patient, and wait for God's timing in your life, just as Jesus had to wait for God's final answer to his prayer at the rock of decision. He had to wait and endure the present in order to enjoy the future.

What did those demons see?

What did the righteous dead see?

What are those around you seeing when the Father asks you to wait, to endure?

What do you see with your eye of faith when you find the Scriptures that promise your deliverance and you pray believing and determined to stand, and nothing seemingly happens?

Keep your eyes upon Jesus because as He knew and knows the end from the beginning, so do we. It's in the book! The Bible already tells us we win. We overcome. We rule. We reign.

The Father wipes away all tears. We are filled with joy. We see our beloved departed ones. We are victorious. Praise God in everything! Everything! Everything!

And Jesus waits, endures, and trusts the Father.

"Our Father which art in heaven, hallowed be thy name."

Questions:

1. I am given the free will right to choose heaven or hell, what is my choice?
2. Am I willing to accept Jesus's sacrifice, which has paid for my unrighteousness, and accept as God's gift His righteousness?
3. Am I now willing to wait for God's perfect timing in my life?
4. Do I believe Jesus won the victory for me? That I am now a winner?

Activity:

Walk an hour alone with God, and listen to his voice, then obey.

CHAPTER 12

THE GLORY BEYOND SCRIPTURE

Apparent defeat always comes before victory. Total submission to the Father is always followed by exaltation and honor from Him. Total trust in the Father is always rewarded. Jesus spoke the words of the Father and did the deeds of the Father:

> *Then said Jesus unto them, When ye have lifted up the Son of man, then shall ye know that I am he, and that I do nothing of myself; but as my Father hath taught me, I speak these things.*
>
> *And he that sent me is with me: the Father hath not left me alone; for I do always those things that please him. (John 8:28–29)*

Then He trusted the Father completely. When we do that, God is honor and word bound to perform His words. We need to seek God's Word for the victories we need in our lives. "Speak the word only, Jesus."

The centurion answered and said, Lord, I am not worthy that thou shouldest come under my roof: but speak the word only, and my servant shall be healed. (Matt. 8:8)

I will trust you to do whatever is necessary to perform your word even if you have to create it.

My covenant will I not break, nor alter the thing that is gone out of my lips. (Ps. 89:34)

For three long days and nights heaven stood still. No angelic choirs sang the praises of God. No cherubim singing "Holy, holy, holy" were heard. The chorus from Bethlehem's hill was silent.

God the Father waited. The price had to be paid. This thing of sin had to be dealt with and settled once and for all. God the Son was doing His part. The Father and the Holy Spirit could only wait.

Just as the Holy Spirit had hovered over the earth at the time of creation, waiting for God the Father to say, "Light be."

And the earth was without form, and void; and darkness was upon the face of the deep. And the Spirit of God moved upon the face of the waters.

And God said, Let there be light: and there was light. (Gen. 1:2–3)

So now He was hovering over the throat of hell, waiting. He was ready for the command He knew was coming, the command for the light of the world to be, again.

Satan and his cohorts had been enjoying the torture of their prize occupant and had brought him out of his cell daily to parade him through the corridors of hell while demons and the damned alike spewed vile and putrid tirades of venom at him. "If you be the Christ, save thyself and us!"

If he had heard that challenge spoken in jeering unbelief once, he had heard it a thousand, nay, a million times. There was no rest, no sleep. Every hour, on the hour, when the gong was sounded to remind his guests where they were, Satan would shout down to the guards, "Is he still there?" The reply, "Yes, master," would bring a roar of laughter that ricocheted off hell's walls with an echo of ungodliness that chilled the stoutest heart and caused knees to buckle and hands and lips to tremble.

In Abraham's bosom, the saints were questioning. "Father Abraham, is it over? Has evil won?"

To all inquiries, Abraham said quietly and simply, "I believe God and His promise. He will not fail. He will not break his covenant."

With hopeful heart, he kept his eye on the promise of the Messiah, though he could not see him.

Michael the Archangel had not taken his eyes off the Father since that moment on earth when heaven went on hold, 3:00 p.m. Wednesday, Jerusalem time, on Golgotha's hill, the time of the Passover sacrifice. Now it was almost sunset on the Sabbath following, and Michael saw the faintest of movements of the Father's head.

The Father had turned away from them all when His Son died and had not moved, until now. One angel said he thought he had heard the Father cry. Oh, the awful price of sin. Someone had to pay it. The unrepentive sinner pays for it in hell. The redeemed pay for it by accepting Jesus as their redeemer and accepting as fact that He paid the full price on the cross.

The faintest of nods caused the heavenly hosts to tune up and then and then...

Oh, look out! It is happening! Almighty God, He who made all there is through his Son, stands to his feet, and with a voice that shook the universe, causing stars to shudder and planets to seek a hiding place, He said, *"It is finished! Holy Spirit, fly into hell and fill my son with my power, then stand aside and watch him do what only a mighty God can do!*

No sooner had He spoken those words when all heaven burst into song. It was a new song the Father Himself had written, and He joined in and sang the song to his son.

The silence has ended!

The rejoicing has begun!

The devil is defeated!

Jesus has won!

The pain of the loss has been replaced with the joy of victory!

God is exalted, and Jesus *is* Lord!

As the Holy Spirit enters into Jesus again, the weak became strong and burst the chains that bound him, tore the gate from its hinges, and He flew straight up to Satan, grabbed him, and whipped him. Then running through the hallways of hell, He made an open show of him, showing all his demons what a weak, puny, puffed-up, toothless lion he really is.

Then He threw that old serpent, the devil in a heap in a corner of hell, and said, "There is your hero! A nothing, a wind! I have even taken away the keys to hell, death, and the grave! He'll not defeat my people anymore!"

With a bound and a spring in His step, He leaped over the chasm separating hell from Abraham's bosom and preached what must be the world's shortest sermon. He said, "I am!"

The Bible tells us He led captivity, captive, or in other words He is about to take all the Old Testament saints to heaven to meet the Father. There are two stops that must he made along the way. Remember He stopped to talk to Mary Magdalene before he went to see the Father?

Jesus saith unto her, (Mary Magdalene) Touch me not; for I am not yet ascended to my Father: but go to my brethren, and say unto them, I ascend unto my Father, and your Father; and to my God, and your God. (John 20:17)

And also the Bible says the following:

And the graves were opened; and many bodies of the saints which slept arose,

And came out of the graves after his resurrection, and went into the holy city, and appeared unto many. (Matt. 27:52–53)

Well, how did this happen? And who were these people? These were some of the souls Jesus was taking to heaven. How surprised would you have been to have a loved one who had been dead for years, showing up at your door telling you he was on his way to heaven with Jesus and it was time for you to accept Him as the Messiah?

Then the grand finale of the old covenant. Jesus, followed by this great cloud of witnesses (saints), enter heaven to watch as Jesus purifies the heavenly mercy seat in the holy of holies with his blood. Have you ever considered the sin of Adam was so far reaching that it spoiled the holiness of the heavenly holy of holies? Well, it did, and only the blood of Jesus could take away that stain and therefore allow sinful man to walk into heaven with full access to God the Father. Amen, hallelujah, praise be to God forevermore!

Neither by the blood of goats and calves, but by his own blood he entered in once into the holy place, having obtained eternal redemption for us. (Heb. 9:12)

Here's how I see the scene:

The Father is waiting, searching the heavenly skyway for his son. At last He sees Jesus, followed by a great company of saints, and he says to his angels, "Bring forth the royal robes, and a ring for His finger, shoes for His feet! This my son was dead and is alive forevermore!

The Father runs to meet his son. There are hugs and kisses, and they dance a jig of joy and sing the Fathers new song to His son. Then Jesus says, "Father, welcome Adam, your first son!"

Stop! Push the Pause button in your mind!

Think about it. God had created Adam and Eve, experienced a joy and fellowship only a parent can feel, the joy of children. Eden in the cool of the day. A perfect place for the perfect couple, the under rulers of God. The god of the earth, created just a shade lower than God Himself.

> *For thou hast made him a little lower than the angels,* (the translators translated the word *Elohim* to angels rather than God as they did in all other times), *and hast crowned him with glory and honour. (Ps. 8:5)*

What joy, what pleasure for them all. God had His angels sure, but they were sealed unto Him after Lucifer's fall, so they had no choice, they had to serve Him. But His man could choose to serve or not to serve Him.

Nothing gives me greater parental pleasure than having one of my children desire my counsel, and I receive my similitude of fatherhood from my Heavenly Father. Oh, the joy He felt as He walked and talked with his son and his son listened.

But and here is a truth for God and man: the greater the love, the greater the risk of hurt. To open oneself up to completely give and receive love makes us vulnerable to the greatest kind of hurt. All through the Old Testament God equates idolatrous Israel to an unfaithful wife. The greatest hurt any human can experience is the discovery that their mate, the one who lies by their side at night and the one with whom the most sacred secrets and fears are shared, has violated their vows and lain with another. God says the pain He feels because of idol worship that is loving anything or anybody more than God is this kind of hurt, and it is what he felt in the garden of Eden. Yet He is love, and therefore, His response is much different than yours or mine might be. He not only forgave them but also went a step further and made a way for complete reconciliation by offering and giving His own life for the ones He loved.

Then He even killed one of His own creations to cover their sin, knowing that a complete removal of the stain left by the sin would have to wait for the sacrifice of God, the Son. So all through the centuries, God, who has everything and is everything, could not have the one thing he had made His finest and final creation for: communion with and companionship with His man. He could not even receive him in His glory when he died, because of sin. Therefore, because of their sin, God had to suffer separation from His son Adam.

Okay, you can start the action again. Push the button.

God the Father turns and sees a perfect Adam and Eve again, hugs them, and says, "Welcome home, children. Welcome home!"

Questions:

1. Have I considered the pain God experienced to give me the gift of reconciliation?
2. Have I thanked him for his gift?
3. Have I given him the only thing he wants from me, me?

Activities:

Activity 1

Friend, if you haven't accepted the gift of salvation through Jesus's sacrifice, do it now. Pray this prayer:

Lord Jesus, I accept you as my Savior right now. I ask you to come into my heart and make me like you. I ask you to forgive me of my sins. I believe God raised you from the dead, and I confess you as my Lord and Savior today. Amen.

Activity 2

If you haven't committed, submitted and given all to Jesus, do it now. Pray this prayer:

Father, I surrender all. I commend to you my spirit, soul, and body. From this day forward, I offer myself a living sacrifice to you and commit to live my life for Jesus, who is now my Lord and Master, amen.

I accept my part of the covenant, Jesus, even unto death.

As I was writing this book and was at the point where Jesus is being helped to walk through the garden, I suddenly heard this in my spirit:

> It's three o'clock
> On Golgotha's Hill,
> The Son of God Died,

All Heaven Stood Still!

I said, "Lord, are you wanting me to write a poem, and this is the beginning?" I laid down my tablet and picked up another one, and I began to write. It took about five minutes to complete, and after I read it, I only had to change one word for it to be complete.

I wept all the while I was writing it, and most people do the same as they read it. I often tell people that I am a scribe, God is the author. I just write what I hear.

CHAPTER 13

WHEN HEAVEN STOOD STILL

It's three o'clock
On Golgotha's Hill,
The Son of God Died,
All Heaven Stood Still!

The Father Turned,
His Head in His Hands,
The Silence was Deafening,
No Angelic Bands.

The Father's Command
Rang Thru Heaven's Halls;
"While My Son's In Hell
Be Silent, One And All!"

Where Are The Heralders,
The Singers of Joy?
Stop What You're Doing,

The Father Grieves For His Boy!

The Angels Were Startled,
Watching The Essence of Love
Cease All His Doings,
He Even Silenced The Dove.

One Angel Was Sure When
Father Knew Jesus Died,
His Shoulders Slumped Over,
And It Looked Like He Cried!

It All Seemed So Eerie
All Heaven So Stilled,
Never Heard Such Silence,
The Fathers Joy Had Been Killed!

The Penalty Of Sin
Became All To Clear,
The Wages Are Death!
Sin's Not Allowed Here.

Oh, Man, Can You See
God's Ultimate Plan
Was To Pay Sins Price,
Then Order Its Ban.

Now The Time Of Completion
Of All That Is True,
Is One Minute Away,
The Son's Suffering, Through!

The Father Stands Up!
Turns His Face Around.
His Eyes Red With Tears,
With His Fist, He Pounds!

"It's Over! It's Finished!
Heavens Justice Is Paid!
Man Is Redeemed,
Salvation's Foundation Laid!"

"I Command You Holy Spirit
Fly Into Hell
Fill My Son With Your Fullness!"
"Angels, Begin Ringing The Bells!"

"Angelic Choirs, Rejoice,
Sing Loud And Sing Clear,
My Son Who Was Dead, Lives!
Satan's Defeat Is Assured!"

Just The Voice Of The Father
Split Open Hell's Walls,
And Jesus Burst Forth
All Humanity To Tell!

But First, He Grabbed Satan,
That Snake, The Ole Devil,
And Whipped Him Completely,
In Front Of All Evil.

He Openly Shamed Him
In Front Of His Clan,
Then Stripped Him Of Keys,
To Give Back To His Man.

He Stepped O'r The Gulf,
Into Abraham's Domain,
And Preached A Short Sermon
He Said *"I Am!"*

Then Led Captivity,
Captive To Earth
To Show Death's Control
Would Now Live In Dearth.

No More Death To The Saint!
God's Grace Is Revived!
By Dying To Christ,
We Are Forever Alive!

The Voice of the Son
Caused the Earth to quake.
Graves opened, Spirits entered,
Dead Saints of Jesus spake.

Then Jesus led all
To enter Heavens Throne,
To present to The Father
All Saints, with sin gone.

A Climax for The Father
Had Finally Come,

Jesus Paid the Price
For Father, to Welcome Son.

"I'm Home Father!
The ordeal is Done!"
With Tears and A Hug,
God said, *"Adam, My Son!"*
(John Dumke, 12/13/95)

CHAPTER 14

FINALE

The angels were waiting outside the heavenly boardroom while a conference goes on between the Father, the Son, and the Holy Spirit. The last meeting of this importance was held just before the earth was prepared for God's man after the fall of Satan and the first destructive flood. This one was a conformation meeting and strategy session for the new and changed ministry of the Man Christ Jesus, the second person of the Godhead, and the Holy Spirit.

The agenda looked like this:

1. Jesus's immediate forty-day ministry on earth.
2. Jesus final instructions to be given to His disciples and His ascension.
3. The Holy Spirit's Pentecost arrival and continued earthly ministry.
4. Jesus ministry of intercession with the Father on behalf of all believes at the Father's right hand.
5. The dispensation of Grace until the time of the Gentiles (nations) be completed.
6. The rapture of the body of believers.
7. The second Advent. The battle and victory at Armageddon.

8. The millennial reign of Jesus Christ from His throne in Jerusalem.
9. The final destiny of Satan at the end of the millennium.
10. The final home of God and man, the new heavens and the new earth ruled from the New Jerusalem.

As the meeting comes to an end Jesus speaks.

"Then it is agreed. I now have all power in heaven and earth, and I am to give the authority to use this power to all that believe on me and confess me as Lord. They will be saved for all eternity and will be free from the curse of the law. They will be at peace with us because I paid the price for all sin for all time. They will be part of our family, with all-family rights and privileges and will have instant access to the throne room and you, Father, through my name. Your Holy Spirit will fill all who ask with power and might."

They held each other's hands and said in unison,

"Amen! So Be It! I Swear It By Me!"

Glorify

I Chose today to glorify you,
To sing a song of praise.
To seek your presence and your face,
My hands, my voice, to Heaven raise.

It makes no difference where I am,
Or what is happening to me,
Whether gladness or sadness, pleasure or pain,
It's in your will to seek to be.

I love you lord, I always will,
I'll follow where're you go.

And if my road is steep and hard,
You'll be right there your strength to show.

I am so blessed. I know 'tis true,
That neither drought nor flood,
Will stay your hand or blessings sure,
For all was paid by Calvary's blood

So, let me say, Christ Jesus,
My savior and my lord,
I chose today to Glorify you,
God's word, my two-edged sword.
(3/12/96)

CONCLUSION
YOUR RESPONSE TO GOD'S CALL

What is your decision? Will you accept God's gift of redemption through Jesus Christ His Son and our Savior?

Or are you going to keep yourself on the throne of your life and separate yourself from God in this life and beyond?

The decision is yours, but here is that simple prayer of acceptance and submission printed for you again, so you can speak it out, believe in your heart and begin your new life in Jesus.

> Lord Jesus, I accept you as my savior right now. I ask you to come into my heart and make me like you. I ask you to forgive me of my sins. I believe God raised you from the dead, and I confess you as my Lord and Savior today. Amen.
>
> Father, I surrender all. I commend to you my spirit, soul, and body. From this day forward, I offer myself a living sacrifice to you and commit to live my life for Jesus, who is now my Lord and Master. Amen."

I accept my part of the covenant, Jesus, even unto death.

Father, into your hands I commend my spirit, soul, and body. Your will for me is what I want, and I trust you completely to do what is for my good and your glory. Amen.

Blessings to all,
John

ACKNOWLEDGMENT

Thank you to a special group of people who helped me complete this book:

Sarah Jenkins:

My editor, who types much faster and better than me, and whose advice, encouragement, and counsel were one of the reasons I was able to complete this work.

Bill Sapp:

Bill's financial support made it possible for me to take the time needed for research and meditation for finishing this project.

Allen C. Dumke:

My brother: What can I say? He is a spiritual giant, blessing all whom he meets and guides in their spiritual walk. He provided financial support, encouragement, and brotherly love.

Frank Easton:

A friend, a partner in business, a real and strong child of the living God. I sent him my manuscript, asking him to call me after he read it. Several hours later, (I wasn't expecting to hear from him for several days), he called. He was so moved he was weeping. I knew that now was the time to move forward and get it published.

Aaron Morse:

Aaron is the angel God sent to me when I was in prison. He made sure the other inmates neither harmed me nor harassed me. He made sure he became my cell mate so we could minister to each other. He is still my angel and friend.

Kent Axtel:

Kent and I have known each other for almost forty years, and during that time, he has taught me much about the moving of the Holy Spirit and the baptism of the Holy Spirit. He is a true spiritual brother in Christ.

Thank you, and blessing to one and all for your kindnesses and support.